WISDOM OF THE TOGA

WISDOM OF THE TOGA

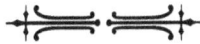

Mythic Patterns That Shape Our Lives

MONICA DAVIS

ISBN-10: 0615716814
ISBN-13: 978-0615716817

CONTENTS

WISDOM OF
THE TOGA

SYMBOL OF THE TOGA

"Lords of the world, and the nation of the toga" was how Virgil, acclaimed first century BCE poet, described the Romans. At the peak of its glory the borders of the Roman Empire stretched from the British Isles into the upper regions of Africa, through Europe, and across the Middle East; with trade routes spreading into India and China. Assimilated cultures were blended and infused with the Romans' native character; integrating hundreds of languages, religions, and beliefs under one unified power—establishing an empire that would define our lives as it swept across time.

Toga was a symbol of Roman citizenship, an outer garment worn for public display, donned not for comfort but for status; each style told its tale. Threads spun from fleece, skillfully woven into cloth, provided warmth and protection from the elements. Each finished cloth was sectioned, then folded over and expressly draped about the body in a deliberate manner. The story of the man wrapped beneath its folds whispered as the gathers of the flowing fabric brushed against history. In ancient Rome, clothes "made the man".

Toga was used as a covering during sleep and as a shroud in death. The countless who displayed this outer garment chronicled the tale of their lives through the recognizable style of its drapery:

- Undyed wool, off-white in color, was used to make the "toga virilis"; a customary style worn by citizen class males from puberty onward.
- The artificially whitened "toga candida" stood out in a crowd; symbolizing the pure and honorable intentions of those political candidates it covered.
- Variations of the "toga praetexta", off-white with a purple border, heralded its wearer as senator or magistrate.
- Cloth dyed a royal purple and ornately decorated with gold embroidery formed the "toga picta"; a style first worn by victorious generals during triumphal processions, and later adopted as the dress donned by emperors for official stately affairs.
- Among the courtly wardrobe hung three colorful "toga trabea": a solid purple (purpura) worn by emperors; a purple or off-white with purple stripes worn by early kings; and a purple adorned with saffron that was reserved for

augurs, the official advisors and interpreters of omens.

- Females were identified through unique styles of their own. Married women wore the "stola", a feminine fashion proclaiming marital status; while adulterous women and prostitutes wore a poorer version of a man's simple toga as a public symbol of shame.
- In times of mourning, a dark colored "toga pulla" was worn to proclaim the wearer's sorrowful message.

People of many ancient cultures dressed in toga-like garments; from plain loose-fitting tattered wraps of common man to exquisitely fashioned and elaborately trimmed robes of rank and royalty. Toga's layered nuances and intricate details cloaked an inner brilliance, passion, and imagination which has captivated the world for thousands of years. It's style fashioned our existence through the actions, and wisdom, of those clothed within its symbol—from philosophers and sages of old, to hopeful school graduates and judges of the Supreme Court.

Hidden beneath its folds are the toga wearers' stories of triumph and despair, conquest and suppression, discovery and achievement; unraveling through time as if by design. Woven throughout historical adventures are mythic patterns that shape our lives; a common thread of humanity. Ancient tales layered in dust, countless adaptations, missing chapters, and loose interpretations conceal clues to an astonishing journey. A developing civilization left a trail of footprints for all to follow; a universal bond that is...the wisdom of the toga.

CHAPTER ONE

THE ETERNAL THREAD OF STORY

The same ideas, one must believe, recur in men's minds
not once or twice, but again and again
~ Aristotle

S tory is the age-old teacher. It is the overlapping common bond among cultures; that which breathes life into being. Stories touch us in a way which deepens our perception of the possible, and offers a glimmer of hope. Perhaps there truly is magic in the world. If we stretch our imagination (and stand on our tiptoes) we may capture a bit of the fantasy which leaves us spellbound…if only for a little while. In the creative realm of storytelling anything is possible, for everything there is, in the moment, real.

Extraordinary ideas travel the currents of time like actors in search of their next great role. Inspired thoughts hover in the air and settle on the tip of the tongue, float along memorable songs, and swirl through the ages on leaves of enduring story. These spirited musings edge their way ever closer, perched on the brink of the present moment, awaiting the sighting of their next destined jumping off point. Sensing their stage of greatest impact they seize an opportunity and glide freely toward their momentary spotlight of discovery.

As inklings of innate notion they drift into our thoughts and rest on our mind as gently as a feather on a pillow. Some of us feel no more than a soft ripple as they pass by and settle unnoticed, while others of us roll over and are tickled in such a way we feel an urgency to awaken, bolt forth, and give shape and form to these visitors from time eternal.

Standing before us as naked truths these changelings quickly uncover the plot in their newly found story and don the appropriate costume; well-rehearsed for their grand entrance in this latest adaptation of "long ago and far away". As players in the everyday dramas of our mundane lives they seek not glory, but rather the gift of aliveness breathed in from the intoxicatingly fresh air of the present moment. Fitting together pieces of this ever expanding puzzle started "once upon a time", each generation, each era contributes in molding the final masterpiece to a yet incomplete whole.

Answers to humankind's age old questions: "Whence came you?" and "Whither art thou bound?", echo beyond our reach; calling out: "All knowledge that was, is now, and will be, already exists.". Traversing time and space we are interconnectedly guided thinkers; acting independently, maneuvering our way along the same path, separated in existence by one another's footprints. Knowledge, remembered and that yet to be remembered, lies dutifully waiting to be summoned like servant by master. We resonate with a peculiar familiarity amassed eons ago, an energy rooted deep within our collective ancestral soul. Bits and pieces of this conscious and unconscious knowing are aroused and pressed into service each and every moment of our lives. Seemingly fresh ideas, mundane discoveries, masterpieces, sheer genius and utter madness are inspired from bygone eras and times yet to come.

STORY AND FATE

In Greek mythology the Moirai are the Fates holding the power to determine what is ordained for each individual, from birth to death. Clotho, the "Spinner", spins the thread which begins the life story; Lachesis, the "Apportioner", carefully measures the length of thread allotted for each person's life; and Atropos, the "Inevitable", cuts the thread at life's end. Like a tailor uses craftsman's tools to skillfully alter a garment we guide our instrument of free will to nip and tuck our fate into a unique and fitting destiny. This becomes our story. We can no more escape participating in life's story than we can escape our own shadow. Each person, and every thing fulfills a perfectly cast role within this divinely costumed, wondrously scripted, and cleverly improvised earthly show of shows.

The guiding spirit of a storyteller grasps hold of our common thread and pulls us in, weaving back and forth; enchanting us with soulful tales of creative discovery. Wonder, illusion, anticipation, and excitement engross us as innovative ideas appear to be pulled out of thin air by these masterfully gifted magicians of words. A twist of phrase, a subtle nuance, an unexpected angle confounds the mind with a whirlwind of possibilities. Unsure of what lies ahead but yearning to know how it all ends, curiosity nudges us forward. With childlike innocence we take a deep breath and dive into the story, embarking on an adventure which carries us throughout this universe and into the next, rediscovering old and uncovering new; trusting the storyteller will guide us safely home.

The Fates pattern life, but it is through our shared individual experiences that we create the strength and richness of a common thread of humanity; a story which binds us to one another as gravity holds us to earth; extending from the beginning of time and ending we know not when. Our threads weave in and out, overlapping and blending as new lives begin and others end. Assuredly we pass through pleasant stretches, gliding along a harmoniously braided measure—our Goldilocks respite—where the thread is neither too loose nor too taut, but just right. Blind faith and stubborn determination move us beyond darkness as we gingerly make our way through frayed spans, hoping they do not unravel before we are across.

Absorbed in the magic of the moment, from "once upon a time" to "happily ever after" completes its journey much too soon, while from "long ago and far away" to "the end" seems to take an eternity as we anxiously await an outcome. Just as we catch our breath and exhale a sigh of relief, we are whisked away from a familiar setting to discover still more pieces of the puzzle; scenes reflecting choices played out in our own storyboard of daily life. Cleverly maneuvering our way through adventures, challenges, and opportunities we face distractions that slow us down and shortcuts to speed us along as we test our resolve in a struggle against ourselves.

The thread of Fate cannot be cut by humankind, but it can be twisted and used against us by our own actions. An individual strand of thread is pliable; it can be wound around, woven in and out, secured to itself, or attached to something else. It can be strengthened yet remain flexible by taking up the slack and folding a single strand over upon itself, or by adding other strands to it. But a rigid thread given limited purpose can be dangerous. Strengthened thread, loosely directed or misguided, can be formed into the hangman's noose; crafting our own demise. Each life is a thread, a story woven into the whole of humankind to create a patterning of history. Each person's daily thoughts and actions contribute to a bond of cooperative strength; or one of misplaced resistance. All experiences play out precisely as they should, custom tailored by our conduct. It is within our grasp to thoughtfully call forth the knowledge of the ages and guide the thread, striking a balance and finding harmony between extremes.

STORY AND MEMORY

The savvy storyteller pulls the thread along, crossing between the worlds of make-believe and everyday life; changing our perspective from observer, to player, to storyteller. The symbolic thread looms before us all; in some it touches a place of genius. A storyteller weaving between worlds, Thomas Edison's concept of a lightbulb moved from an idea, into the tangible world as a device illuminating surroundings, and back to thought...as a universally-accepted symbol for a flash of genius...an "Aha Moment" pictured as a lightbulb above the head...an inspired remembering. It was through the use of carbonized cotton thread that Edison was able to create a filament...a glowing thread.

History carries examples of thread used to remember "something". The Book of Genesis tells of the birth of twins sired by Judah and carried by Tamar. The midwife tied a scarlet thread around the wrist of the first born as a means to quickly identify who was the eldest child. We symbolically "tie a string around a finger" as a memory aid. Remembering names, places, and dates provides assurance, and offers hope that we might fulfill our social need to maintain a bond to someone or something beyond ourselves. The precious gift of conscious remembering, to relive moments and reconnect with familiar stories, defines the very essence of our being. Without it we lose perspective on experiences which carry the understanding to develop true wisdom.

We face two demons of memory. Amnesia steals our gift of times past, and dementia cruelly pushes us into a progressive madness—one which slowly loosens our hold on recollections of a familiar world. We seek innovative ways to ward off these evil demons by improving our memory; exercising the brain by stretching and reaching for new ways to strengthen the tie to our perception of reality. Seeking ways to keep the memory intact, to differentiate between subjective familiarity and distorted illusion has been an age old quest. Preliterate cultures combined oral communication with common associations to carry instruction, spread beliefs, and preserve history. Thousands of years ago the ancient Greeks turned to the power of story, creating wondrous mythical tales. The Titaness Mnemosyne, goddess of memory and remembrance, remains rooted in time, offering assistance through the word "mnemonic". A mnemonic device triggers recall by jogging the memory, tugging on a thread to our past, illuminating a lightbulb of remembrance. Invoking a mnemonic device sends a cosmic vibrational ping of sorts, echoing back to ancient Greece, calling forth the aid of Mnemosyne.

Effective memory techniques borrow from poetic storytelling; wrapping important concepts within rhythm, rhyme, and alliteration. An example of a common spelling aid taught to modern-day school children is the rhyming verse: "'I' before 'E', except after 'C', or as sounded like 'AY' as in neighbor or 'weigh'". This particular mnemonic applies two key elements—rhythm and rhyme—to help us first remember its catchy melodic verse, and then trigger recall of the lesson within that saying. A wonderful concept; a flawed lesson. (Not all word spellings follow this rule: "weird" and "science" are two such exceptions.)

Stories are universal mnemonics; common threads of communication. Where better to store messages for safekeeping than in melodic and descriptive tales? Successful use of story as a long-term method of delivery for reliable information, or to maintain continuity of societal structure across vast geographic boundaries was no easy task. It required keeping the essence of the message intact. Ancient storytellers were skillful, using utmost care to preserve and treasure the values passed along from person to person, generation to generation.

Ancient Greeks called on the goddess Mnemosyne for her help in assuring a smooth and accurate recitation. Homer's epic poems: *The Iliad* (siege of Troy), *The Odyssey* (journey of Odysseus), and the *Homeric Hymns* (short poems paying tribute to godly beings), are significant works of oral recording believed to contain historical events. Preserving their content required careful recitation, so as not to alter the facts of history to any great degree.

Yet, the charm in oral storytelling is from the added flavor sprinkled in by each individual style; a slight embellishment or play on words which creates a signature unique to a particular storyteller. Balance must be reached. Accomplished storytelling captivates an audience, reaching deep into one's imagination to mesmerize and conjure; painting pictures through words and expression. How we absorb, remember, translate, and apply the knowledge of the ages is what distinguishes us one from another; and determines the very framework of our lives.

ARCHETYPES

S tories apply metaphor, figures of speech and symbolism, to emulate fundamental principles. One need look no further than familiar characters who serve as reminders of the ancient teachings; tales casting heroes and villains in roles of victory or demise. These surface roles carry deeper meanings, blending and interweaving...forming archetypes. Archetypes represent an innate collection of commonly shared experiences; universal references which serve the broader needs of humankind. The term "archetype" was popularized in modern psychology usage by Carl Jung, noted 20th century Swiss psychiatrist. Jung suggested archetypes as roles or personalities within us which play out; called forth at various times in our lives.

Drawn from an array of archetypal labels and variations we masterfully slip into whichever guise enables us to act out our current drama: nurturing parent, helpless child, damsel in distress, hero rescuer, warrior, mediator, teacher, student; quickly tailoring our behavior to suit the scenario. Openly projecting an assortment of roles adds emphasis and depth to our actions, like actors change costumes and demeanor to reflect the persona of their current character portrayal.

We don archetypes as if they were theater costumes sewn from a collection of threads. Strung together to form a useful and well-designed whole, a story is told through each shifting pattern. Fashioned in one way the colorful threads tell of a medieval jester's fated life, outwardly exhibiting merrymaking while masking an inner humility; forced to perform from beneath the costume of a fool. Alter the garment and the threads may tell the romantic tale of an elegant party dress swept up in the movements of a young woman who wears it on her most joyous occasion. Look closely and those very threads bear the tales collected from the ancient toga of a wise old sage; carried forward on the winds of time.

THEORIES OF MYTH

Mythic patterns began unfolding with the telling of the very first story. Author Thomas Bulfinch, in his mid 19th century work, *Age of Fables*, spoke of four philosophical theories on the origin of myth: Scriptural, Historical, Allegorical, and Physical. The Scriptural theory asserts that all myths have a basis in Sacred writings, but the facts and characters have been altered and colored. Historical theory holds that characters were once real human beings and their mythical stories are time-layered glorifications of the facts. The Allegorical theory supposes myths are figurative and symbolic, contain a moral or a belief, and may be based on a factual event or person. The Physical theory proposes the natural elements of air, fire, and water became objects of devotion and religious worship through creation of divine beings, as personifications of Nature. (Do we not still make reference to "Mother" Nature and understand perfectly well the significance of her mighty power?)

Artful storytelling weaves through time stitching together bits and pieces from each of these theories. Tailoring the pattern to suit its audience, it fashions a colorful and fitting message to drape about the shoulders of humanity. Exploring myth creation and the captivating world of storytelling provides clues to a greater understanding of our vast universe. An accomplished storyteller moves beyond literal interpretation to engulf the true essence of the deeper meaning. The many forms through which the message may be delivered: oral, written, acted, sculpted—fiction or fact—is but the doorway to what lies beyond; a multifaceted journey affirming an age old lesson.

The ancients dispensed wise counsel through an elixir of storytelling; prolonging and preserving precious bits of life to be rediscovered, retold, adapted, and infused with insight and foresight. Masterful and meticulous in their delivery, these caretakers of the soul skillfully measured out a healthy balance of historical fact mixed with imaginative fantasy. Swirled together and swallowed down with a strong dose of heartwarming entertainment, it is the remedy that awakens the magic within us all, calling forth the knowledge of the ages that has always been. Follow the eternal thread of story, and with the blessing of Mnemosyne, humankind's fate will be remembered, and a glorious destiny created.

CHAPTER TWO

REMEMBERING BACK

History is the witness that testifies to the passing of time;
it illumines reality, visualizes memory, provides guidance
in daily life and brings tidings of antiquity
~ Marcus Tullius Cicero

Astonishing tales of gods and monsters, strange and wonderful lands, heroic deeds and fierce battles were created during a period when some of the most illuminating and imaginative minds lived. It was a time when names carried the description of a larger than life persona: Alexander the Great, a king of Macedon and conqueror of the Persian Empire; and Ptolemy Soter (the "Savior"), who was credited with building to greatness the ancient library of Alexandria.

It was a time of Aesop and his fables; Herodotus, the "father of history"; Euripides and his dramatic theatrical tragedies; Hippocrates, the "father of western medicine"; and

Pythagoras, a man identified with his contribution to mathematics, the Pythagorean theorem.

The classical Greek philosopher Socrates was known (and condemned) for his creative process of opening one's mind to a realm of greater possibilities. He engaged in a questioning dialogue to uncover potential weaknesses in beliefs, contradictions, and conclusions. This form of critical thinking, called the Socratic Method, survived the ages and is used in classrooms at modern day universities.

METAPHOR AND ALLEGORY

Did such a rich culture, steeped in contemplative genius, naively believe that almighty beings existed in the world around them? Far more likely, their deep philosophical understanding led them to create a wondrous world of immortal gods and mythological tales to use as an innovative, brilliantly crafted instructional system; one immersed in metaphor and allegory. Great stories remain in memory, more easily understood, recalled, and recited than boring facts.

The philosopher Plato, in his 4th century BCE work *Republic*, acknowledged the use of allegory and cautioned: "...the battles of the gods in Homer's verse are things that we must not admit into our city either wrought in allegory or without allegory. For the young are not able to distinguish what is and what is not allegory.". Aristotle, a student of

Plato, offered further insight in his work *Poetics*: "But the greatest thing by far is to have command of metaphor. This alone cannot be imparted by another; it is the mark of genius, for to make good metaphors implies an eye for resemblances.".

Nowadays, to hear the casual comment "It's raining cats and dogs" does not make us look skyward with an expectation of seeing household pets falling from the heavens; we understand the phrase to be a metaphor for a heavy downpour. Similarly, George Orwell's *Animal Farm* was not intended as a literal account of farm animals ruling society but, as his original title describes: *Animal Farm: A Fairy Story*. It is an allegory, a political satire using familiar characteristics and parallel thinking to drive home a point.

UNIVERSAL CONCEPTS

Common beliefs are deeply rooted in the collective mind. Although we are independent in our individual expression we are connected to one another through an innate familiarity. Humankind shares among and within us a fundamental conceptual understanding of several key basic themes and ideals. The general concept of beauty for example, whether considered skin deep or in the eye of the beholder, evokes in each of us a pleasing, satisfying sense. How each individual defines beauty is unique to his or her own taste, but we share the impression of a universal perception that true beauty transcends the physical senses and enters into a surreal consciousness, unnecessary (or perhaps impossible) to be verbally described. Art, for example, is beautiful to those in whom it strikes a chord; yet one admirer's beauty may be perceived as grotesquely offensive to another.

Conceptually, love exists as romantic, familial, friendly, playful; love of nature, the arts, life. We may fall in love, be in love; deeply, passionately, lost. Touched by Elizabeth Barrett Browning's sonnet *How Do I Love Thee?* moves us to a place of deep inner reflection; relaxing us into a heartfelt, peaceful sigh. She made no attempt to define "love", for that is a shared knowing within us all. Browning used this sonnet to express her heightened sense of awareness, embodied from personal experience, as she thoughtfully pondered the question, "How do I love thee?".

Her soulful outpouring was accentuated in a brilliantly crafted sonnet, to caress the mind and soothe the heart by its very structure. Browning applied a precise rhythmic pattern of recurring stressed and unstressed syllables, interspersed with rhyme, accompanied by passionate phrasing, and repetition of the word "love" as emphasis. To read her sonnet is to eavesdrop on her most private thoughts; swept up in the moment as the tone resounds in our ears, breathing in her celebration of love.

Sonnets From the Portuguese – Sonnet 43,
by Elizabeth Barrett Browning

How do I love thee? Let me count the ways.
I love thee to the depth and breadth and height
My soul can reach, when feeling out of sight
For the ends of Being and ideal Grace.
I love thee to the level of everyday's
Most quiet need, by sun and candlelight.
I love thee freely, as men strive for Right.
I love thee purely, as they turn from Praise.
I love thee with the passion put to use
In my old griefs, and with my childhood's faith.
I love thee with a love I seemed to lose
With my lost saints,—I love thee with the breath,
Smiles, tears, of all my life!—and if God choose,
I shall but love thee better after death.

+≍ ≍+

The ancients understood that shared ideals formed a foundation for cultural understanding. Common, everyday objects were assigned symbolic representation woven throughout wondrous tales to skillfully enmesh two fundamental memorization techniques—association and imagination. Engaging in rhythmic oral storytelling accompanied by colorful visual imagery evoked a whole-brain approach to learning. One part of the brain analyzes, processes and catalogs words, numbers and symbols; another part sees the bigger picture, images and patterns, gestures and movement to create a complete reference.

Hearing artful verse with well-placed dramatic pauses and deliberate inflections opens the senses to flowing, melodic tones which capture our attention and ease memorization. An accomplished storyteller presents events in such a way that our minds observe, recreate, and participate in each picturesque performance. Processing stories using all senses (touch, taste, smell, sight, hearing) strengthens the connection between creative imagination and reality; providing multiple avenues through which to stimulate retention and recall.

Wellthoughtoutdescriptivephrasingengagesthesenses... even in absence of the physical object. One may grasp a basic understanding of a lemon from the sentence: "A small yellow fruit in the citrus family with a refreshingly pleasant fragrance and strong sour flavor.". But a storyteller can create an engaging, sensual experience by describing this same lemon as: "A fruitful golden orb bathed in sunlight, exuding a lively acidic tone to invigorate the nostrils. A small taste from its soft juicy flesh seizes the palate with a tart kiss, as if to steal away all sweetness we have known.". The lemon itself does not have to be physically seen or tasted to stimulate a memory of it...and evoke a physical response of salivation.

GODS AND HEROES

Myths and tales from long ago and far away spread round the globe, spawning cultural variations; each version resonated with the particular group it touched. Ancient storytellers created a shared experience by drawing an audience into the fantasy. Developing a personal attachment to the story enabled the listener to feast on the celebrated victories, and grieve and laugh along with the characters. So deep was their connection that elements of these classic stories were brought to life through physical structures. Skillfully sculpted statues and magnificent shrines, imbued with the energy of past tales, stand as places in which to immerse oneself in the shadows of remarkable adventures.

We are not so different from our ancestors. We too desire to connect to heroic deeds, and acknowledge special beings. We pay homage to our heroes by erecting statues, and carving their names onto buildings. Like the people of ancient cultures who set aside sacred time in which to honor the patronage of their divine beings, we proclaim special dates as memorials; paying tribute to distinguished persons and events.

Does story spin to imitate life, or is humankind's fascination with astonishing tales and inspiring heroes so great that we create deep-seated reminders so as not to forget the lessons within the myths? Developing stories based on cultural truths carves a pathway which traces a timeless link from past to present to future. The Greeks bestowed upon their gods human traits and emotions: anger, sorrow, lust, compassion, loyalty, love, physical strength, and beauty. Mythic characters were deemed wise, clever, cunning, demanding, heartless, empathetic…and flawed.

Hephaestus, god of fire, master of the forge, and artisan blacksmith is described in Theogony by the 8th century BCE poet Hesiod as "the famous Lame One" and "the very famous Limping God". His physical deformity is described in the *Homeric Hymn to Pythian Apollo*, by his mother, Hera: "But my son Hephaestus whom I bare was weakly among all the blessed gods and shrivelled of foot, a shame and a disgrace to me in heaven, whom I myself took in my hands and cast out so that he fell in the great sea.".

Storytellers created Hephaestus less physically perfect than the other Olympians, but justified his place among the gods by blessing him with the gift of extraordinary craftsmanship; a skill through which his noble existence was celebrated. Hephaestus was the symbolic outcast; rejected by his mother, and spurned by lovers. His status as a god elevated the scope of his suffering beyond mortal pain. He endured the personal ache of emotional wounds by channeling his passion into the creation of magnificent artifacts—treasures so splendid they were coveted by the gods themselves. He, the Olympian deemed lesser by physical measure, a failure in love, became highly revered; elevated through glorious perfection in craft.

Aided by the Cyclopes, a race of giants with a single eye in the middle of the forehead, Hephaestus forged the mighty thunderbolts of Zeus, arrows used by Eros (Cupid), the winged helmet of Hermes (Mercury), and the shield of the hero Achilles. His apprentice blacksmith Cyclopes, grotesque in appearance yet skilled in craft, faithfully assisted their crippled, brilliant master. This downtrodden allegiance of beastly underdogs honed their trade on a forge deep within a volcano; far from public scrutiny.

Hephaestus was called Vulcan by the Romans, and his honor as master of the forge continues through that name. "Vulcanization" is a process which uses heat to infuse material with strength, elasticity, and durability. "Volcano" (burning mountain), is an ancient description of Mount Etna on the isle of Sicily, a place the Romans called the forge of Vulcan. Perhaps there is more truth to the story behind a crippled Hephaestus than we know. The blacksmith played a prominent role in ancient cultures; his skills relied on to forge weapons and tools for survival. Those who served as blacksmith were at times deliberately lamed, or shackled with leg irons to prevent them from easily traveling to seek work elsewhere. Could this be a case of story imitating life?

An inkling of Hephaestus, tortured, wounded, misunderstood, exists in us all. The trials and tribulations we face, alone or together, whether viewed as powerful opportunities or cruel obstacles, may be transcended by recognizing the special talent we each possess; a gift within us to be embraced, nurtured, and polished. Only by accepting our weaknesses and honoring our talents can we radiate in the world; seen for our strengths rather than mocked for our flaws.

ADAPTATION OF MYTH

The Roman's conquered, and their empire spread. Time left its mark on humankind, and stories were retold as a blend of assimilated cultures. In present day retelling of myths, Greek and Roman names are commonly interchanged, yet we understand the tale, for we either learned them this way, or have come to accept and embrace the variations. In Greek myths, gods openly associated with mortals; not merely existing "out there" but as part of our world, walking among us, drawing us in until their stories merged with our stories. Tales of gods freely interacting with humankind offered hope that "any man", rather than "no man" or "select man", could have a personal encounter with divine immortality.

Occasionally the gods took mortal partners, producing from those unions the demigods; a race of offspring half mortal, half god. Perseus, who slew Medusa, was son of the god Zeus and the mortal woman Danae. A familiar name among the demigods is that of Hercules. Adaptations (especially movies and television) referred to Hercules as the son of the

Greek god Zeus, but Hercules is his Roman name as son of Jupiter. Heracles is the name given him as son of the Greek god Zeus and the mortal woman Alcmene. The Romans adapted stories from the Greeks and added their own flair; a twist, or some new perspective which made them identifiably Roman. We borrow from the Roman name by ascribing the adjective "herculean" as a characteristic, meaning a daunting task, or something of gigantic proportion.

The gods and demigods were not always noble. Many of the great storied deeds described in tales of Hercules (Heracles) were carried out as atonement for careless and heinous acts he had committed. What we commonly call the "Twelve Labors of Hercules" has been attributed to the works of the 7th century BCE Greek poet Peisander and his stories about Heracles. The "twelve labors" was a sentence of justice handed down by King Eurystheus of Tiryns as punishment after Heracles killed his own family while in a state of temporary insanity cast upon him by Hera.

MODERN-DAY INSPIRATION

One of Heracles's twelve labors was to rid Crete of a savage bull. To capture the bull Heracles fashioned a lasso, threw it over the beast's head, wrestled it down and bound it with rope; then, depending on the version of the story, he either carried or rode the subdued bull back to King

Eurystheus. Now picture this scene forward into present day, as a steer roping rodeo contest. A cowboy (hero) pursues a steer, lassos it with his rope, throws it to the ground and binds together three of its legs.

Envision this scene as another familiar rodeo event...bull riding. A cowboy hero sits atop the animal's back and, holding tightly to the bull rope (a braided cord), quests to ride the menacing beast for 8 seconds. (A much shorter ride than Heracles undertook when he rode the Cretan bull back to Tiryns.) Imagine how these stories of Heracles and his heroic actions, kept alive as memories on our common thread, provided inspiration for the feats of rodeo cowboys.

As heroes of man, demigods added a deeper layer and broader dimension; one which enriched the bond between divine beings of story and the everyday lives of humankind. Enthralled by these godlike beings, we forget, never learn, overlook, or excuse their barbaric actions; choosing instead to accept and emulate their fantastic deeds and heroic feats. In myth the "hero" was the defender and protector. Left vulnerable and exposed, heroes were at times protected and at times attacked by the gods. Heroes endured excruciating agony, but also experienced magical moments. They undertook seemingly insurmountable labors and quests; their epic achievements in league with our own secret Walter Mitty-like dreams of greatness. The lives of ancient humankind aligned with interwoven stories of courageous deeds and daring feats; and the characters evolved. Powers and attributes of gods and heroes were further developed and modified to match the call of the ages. They grew in depth and flourished in story to feed a culture hungry for heroes and legends befitting the times.

PATRONAGE AND TRIBUTES

Storytellers assigned the gods patronage over nearly everything in the universe. Perhaps this was humankind's rationale to relieve accountability; there is less personal pressure when sharing or shifting responsibility, and blame, with divine beings. Offering the will of the gods as explanation for unpleasant occurrences outside the control of "common man" (natural disasters, disease, war, and famine) gave life resolve. Whether believing the gods were doling out punishment against them, or aiding them in glorious victory, anyone could partner with the divine to cope with the harsh realities of life.

Seemingly as a matter of course and convenience, humankind embraced the power of "poetic license" and reassigned patronage among their gods. Powers could be shared or transferred from one god to another merely by adapting a story, or telling a new one. The *Homeric Hymns* describes the sun as the ancient Titan Helios (root of the word "helium"), enlivened in the verse: "Bright rays beam dazzlingly from him, and his bright locks streaming from the temples of his head gracefully enclose his far-seen face: a rich, fine-spun garment glows upon his body and flutters in the wind: and stallions carry him.".

But the Olympian Apollo, god of light, prophecy, and music, was also associated with the sun, and it is Apollo who takes the sun's focus as its central guiding figure in many stories. Both Helios and Apollo were long ago cast in similar roles to paint a picture of the motion of a radiant sun traveling across the sky from morning 'til night. Each, at times, filled the role as the god who drove his golden chariot pulled by solar steeds from Heaven to Ocean in a neverending daily cycle of sunrise and sunset.

Myth adaptation emerged as themes in novels, movies, and television soap operas. We boo our villains, laud our heroes, empathize with their flaws, and honor their strengths. Reveling in this fantasy world gives praise to Phantasos, the ancient Greek deity whose name means to bring images to the mind. He is one of the dream gods known as the Oneiroi. Fantasizing and daydreaming allow us to travel corridors in our minds to a place where we can become immersed and absorbed in our stories; fantastically lost in the moment.

DIVAS AND FANS

At times we blur the line, confusing an actor with their character role. We turn from fans to fanatics, obsessed with following the unfolding story and reliving each moment. We create a fanbase on social networks, and attend fanfests hoping to interact with our modern day heroes; yearning to connect, to share with mythic beings as did those before us.

Ancient humankind offered tribute to gods and heroes of long ago and far away in exchange for favors; blessings and precious gifts of goodwill and approval. So too are "divine beings" of present day paid tribute. Divas from the entertainment industry are acknowledged through applause, accolades, and awards. A stellar performance may be rewarded by a statuette; an idol to behold as an endearing reminder of their acclaim.

The Academy of Motion Pictures Arts and Sciences describes "The Oscar" statuette as: "the most recognized trophy in the world". It's design (by Cedric Gibbon) is described as: "a knight standing on a reel of film gripping a crusader's sword"; a true hero representation. The Hollywood Foreign Press Association presents its recipients with the "Golden Globe", a trophy depicting the world wrapped in filmstrip. The Screen Actors Guild (SAG) honors a select few with "The Actor", a bronze nude male statuette holding the theatrical mask of comedy in one hand and the mask of tragedy in the other. And the Television Academy's Emmy award offers a statuette of a winged woman holding up an atom to represent a Muse of the art and science of television.

So taken are we by awards, prizes, and lavish banquets held to honor excellence, that we celebrate accomplishments in all walks of life—music, sports, business, science…cooking, and spelling. We are not so different from our ancestors, reaching beyond the mundane to achieve something more. We hold onto a glimmer of hope that it is within each of us to earn immortality and receive recognition for our extraordinary feats. Should we stumble, or fall short, we try again. And in the meantime we shall bask in celebration of those who succeed.

CHAPTER THREE

THE LABYRINTH AND THE MAZE

A person often meets his destiny
on the road he took to avoid it
~ Jean de La Fontaine

For thousands of years the labyrinth has captivated cultures; appearing in carvings on rock walls, depicted in artwork, and as imprints on coins. It was designed as a journey of exploration and adventure through intricate passageways with complex twists and turns. The sacred symbol of the labyrinth was inlaid in church floors to serve as a symbolic spiritual pilgrimage; an act of repentance for those who walked its path. A true labyrinth has but a single route leading to its center. To find the way out, continue onward where the path winds back to the beginning and the entrance becomes the exit through which one emerges into a life forever changed.

Born into this world we cast our lot in this game of chance, anticipating a delightful blending of the individual self with that of the broader worldly experience. We enter life's labyrinth bewitched into believing that our fate is one of sacrificial prisoner, a slave to our environment, a victim of circumstance. Upon hearing a faint distant call beckoning to us from within we courageously abandon the illusion of our shackles. Our constraints and limitations become swallowed up by time, dissolved in the warming light of our awakening as we push onward, imposing our free will to fulfill our destiny. Through a series of missteps and right steps we walk life's path, gaining understanding, experience, and wisdom along the way.

THESEUS AND THE MINOTAUR

The mythological tale of Theseus and the Minotaur conjures up images of a perilous adventure; a foreboding death sentence into King Minos's labyrinth for all who faced the abomination of the Minotaur within its walls. Depicted as a creature with the physical head and tail of a bull and the body of a man, the Minotaur was said to be a monster so vile, hideous, and uncontrollable that he was imprisoned deep within the most intricately constructed labyrinth; one designed by the cunning craftsman and skillful architect Daedalus.

King Minos used well his bully the Minotaur to inflict a horrifying punishment upon those by whom he felt wronged. As retribution for the murder of his son Androgeus at the hands of Athenians, King Minos demanded a precious treasure of youthful human sacrifice be paid to Crete as a recurrent tribute. For each payment a number of young Athenian men and women were drawn by lot, carried across the sea in a ship with black sails, and delivered into a grave fate—emboweled within the labyrinth—their flesh torn from them as they were feasted on by the Minotaur.

As these innocent young men and women of ancient Athens were selected by lottery, so too throughout history did humankind institute a military draft; a selective service lottery to determine which of our young men would be offered up, shipped overseas, marched forth and locked in a foreign entanglement to face a stubborn bullheaded foe. Young men of modern times who dared evade their fated voyage abroad did not escape retribution. For these young men (draft dodgers), were subject to banishment from their homeland, or suffered confinement within the humility of our own labyrinth of prisons.

Theseus, hero of this tale and heir to the throne of Athens, volunteered to accompany a group of doomed youths to Crete and vanquish the Minotaur. Upon arriving in Crete, Theseus fortuitously became the object of infatuation for King Minos's daughter Ariadne, who could not bear the thought that she would forever lose him to the belly of the beast. Begging Daedalus for help, Ariadne was given a clew of thread to pass to Theseus…with instructions for him to tie one end at the entrance to the labyrinth and unwind the thread along his path as he journeyed inward.

Theseus entered the labyrinth, cautiously picking his way step by step, unrolling the thread as he traveled deeper into the unknown in search of his foe. Encountering the Minotaur, Theseus, prepared for battle, took the bull by the horns and slay the beast within. Trusting his physical strength and inner courage, with exuberant determination did Theseus recast a victim's fate into a hero's destiny; then followed along the clew of thread stretched before him to safely resurface from the battleground.

CONFRONTING THE BULL(Y)

Tales commonly depict scenes in which one's bravery is tested during confrontation with a bull…or bully… an age old theme carried into life. Ancient artifacts show sketches of men and women engaged in "bull-leaping", an acrobatic sport of courage and agility. As a charging bull approached, a jumper attempted to either grasp the bull's horns like pommels on a gymnastic horse and hurdle over the bull, or land with a handstand on the bull's back and launch into a somersault to safety.

The yearly ritual of the running of the bulls held in Pamplona, Spain has men and women scrambling for their lives alongside angry, confused beasts. It is not uncommon to hear reports of persons who foolishly wandered too close to a charging animal (or were unfortunately herded into its path), getting trampled—"bull-dozed"; seriously injured or killed while participating in this form of ritualistic bravado. The beasts complete their journey through the streets of Pamplona, the passageway of the labyrinth, to face their fate in its center—the sacrificial bullring—where they are ceremoniously slain in sport; imitating a scene from a mythic tale.

Hero confronting bull is exemplified in the sport of bullfighting. The matador, draped in finely tailored costume, cautiously and determinedly enters the ring, keenly aware of the callous danger within. Confidently standing before the beast he holds out a cape woven from the symbolic thread of the hero's clew, and waves it in defiance. There is no turning back, the hero must be victorious or fall victim to his foe in the ring. The piercing eyes of the matador remain fixated on the snorting bull as a cloud of dust swirls from the stomp of its hoof before a charge. Onward, step back, to the side, remain centered; the hero's cape floats across the horns of the enraged bull. The hero continues this dance of confrontation and evasion with the passion of a tango, meeting each pass of the bull with shouts of "Olé", "Bravo"; until, with that final fatal blow, he slays the symbolic beast of the Minotaur.

Having successfully fulfilled his quest, the matador exits the ring, lauded by the crowd's jubilant cheers.

DOUBLE-EDGED SWORD

Like the matador, we may willingly choose risk...but sometimes risk is cast upon us, as if chosen by lot. Rise to hero or fall as victim; two choices, two views, both with ties to ancient myth. The word "labyrinth" has been associated with the weapon "labrys", a double-edged axe; symbol of royal power in ancient Lydia, and an object used in religious ceremonies. It is the instrument depicted in scenes of the Greek goddess Athena's supernatural birth. The double-edged axe was wielded by Hephaestus to strike the blow that split open the head of Zeus; freeing a fully grown, robed and helmet clad Athena, goddess of wisdom and war. Unlike her brother Ares, god of war who thirsts for the thrill of the battle and feeds on its horrors, Athena, protector of heroes and patroness of war, is thoughtful and wise as she guides its course.

Athena's message weighs on us like a coat of armor. From the head a thought is born, an idea with the power to release unconventional wisdom, accompanied by two choices: praise for honorable expression of thoughts and deeds, or criticism for negative action. Split apart by contrasting views we are left victims of our own dual nature; our double-edged sword. An ancient reminder to "think before you act".

Athena gifted the first olive tree to her namesake city, Athens. Winners of the ancient Olympic Games (battles of sport) were crowned with wreaths made of olive branches and leaves. We honor Athena's gift to humankind through symbolically extending an olive branch as a gesture of peace. The emblem of the United Nations displays a map of the world surrounded by two olive branches, signifying a quest for world peace. Athena, born from the mind of Zeus, mighty ruler and god of justice, offers humankind the olive tree as a reminder for us to use our heads, and apply wisdom to discern when the gesture of peace and harmony, rather than conflict and destruction, is the truer path to lasting resolution.

LABYRINTH OR MAZE

With the passage of time comes a blending of attitudes, and a change in perspective. The word "maze" has become interchangeable with "labyrinth"; but unlike the distinction of a true unicursal labyrinth, a maze offers multiple pathways; dead ends, and choices for entrance and exit. The maze is designed as a puzzle to solve, something to reason out; an interactive enigma filled with challenges and opportunities. The labyrinth has but one path leading to its center; the quest to slay the beast and emerge victorious. The maze is multifaceted and engaging, a journey of exploration where we may stumble across an exit before finding the center...

or never find the center. In the maze we take two steps forward and one step back; change course, meander, progress. Our chosen path may lead to a shortened journey, an early exit leaving some paths unexplored. Should the going get tough, change course and explore an easier route.

Following the course of the maze adds complexities, both complicating and enriching our lives. We enter a labyrinth knowing that the path will lead to its center, but the maze is a lesson of uncertain choices. Still, we press onward, eager to delve into its mystery. With joyous anticipation we seek the completion of our journey; for in the maze it is not the threat of the Minotaur lurking in the shadows that must be overcome, we must solve the riddle of the maze itself to fulfill our destiny. We make choices, take action, glance back and wonder, "What if?", "What might have been?" had we chosen to turn a different corner.

The mythic labyrinth was built as a prison. But during the Middle Ages mazes were built for the amusement of royalty and the wealthy. Beautifully fashioned, cut through gardens, they had evolved from the lair of the evil Minotaur to a celebratory place of ritual dance, religious pilgrimage, and joyful frivolity.

Curiosity and amusement envelop us as we walk with childlike wonder through modern-day mazes cut within corn fields; playfully treading through a grain that was our ancestors' precious life sustaining nourishment. As we pick our way through the ears of corn do we hear the ancestral voices carried on the wind, whispering a reminder of its deeper purpose? Or are we deafened by the rustling of the stalks, caught up the bustle of the crowd, intent on playing a game; so lost in the thrill of the moment that not only is the way out hidden from our view, but our own ears are not attuned to the deeper message. We continue onward unaware that the vibration, the energy pattern of the ancient lesson shadows us, nudging us to remember as we brush against the yielding form of its design.

FOLLOW THE YELLOW BRICK ROAD

In L. Frank Baum's story, *The Wonderful Wizard of Oz*, Dorothy followed the hero's clew as she stepped onto the path of "the road of yellow brick". The book describes the land of Oz as surrounded on all sides by a great desert; the City of Emeralds lies: "exactly in the center of the country". When Dorothy asks, "How can I get there?" she is told, "You must walk. It is a long journey, through a country that is sometimes pleasant and sometimes dark and terrible.". In the movie adaptation, released 40 years after the book was published, Dorothy's path along the "Yellow Brick Road" offered a choice, a fork in the road where she first met Scarecrow…a fork not mentioned in the book.

A scene from the book offers opportunity for reflection as it describes the perils of moving thoughtlessly forward. "Scarecrow often stumbled over the yellow bricks, which were here very uneven...broken or missing altogether, leaving holes that Toto jumped across and Dorothy walked around. As for the Scarecrow, having no brains, he walked straight ahead, and so stepped into the holes and fell at full length on the hard bricks." Labyrinth or maze...be this road of yellow bricks? It matters not, for thoughtful awareness and focused attention are necessary to successfully navigate either.

As with many great myths from long ago, the original story of Oz was modified, and retold to play out in a new era; adapted to entice another audience. Had Dorothy chosen to journey down a different fork than the one we watched her select in the movie she may have encountered a series of quite different experiences, met other characters, learned other lessons before arriving, or perhaps never reaching, the Emerald City. Countless untold versions of this and other beloved tales lie along the thread of time, yet to be remembered into being, for stories exist along every pathway.

Stories, whenever, wherever, or however told or retold, are precious gifts to be enjoyed, cherished, and shared. They are subtle reminders that as we live out our own life story, each adventure should be fully experienced, and treasured; for how we adapt in life is uniquely ours.

HERO'S JOURNEY

Joseph Campbell, 20th century mythologist and scholar, described the motif of the "monomyth"; a pattern played out in steps, experienced through a heroic journey. Its three main parts: Departure, Initiation, and Return each contain several stages. The intrigue begins when a hero receives a "call to adventure". Often this first summons is dismissed, but intervening circumstances push the reluctant hero forward...and the adventure begins. Along the way the hero faces obstacles, is occasionally offered divine assistance, relies on his own wits, and becomes wiser from the experience. The hero eventually reaches a treasured goal, gathers up the boon, and makes the return home; victoriously completing the quest.

How fitting that the main character in the tale of Oz is named Dorothy—derived from the Greek "doron" (gift) and "theos" (god). Dorothy and her arduous journey represent each of us, God's gifts on Earth, heroically facing challenges and triumphantly enjoying success as we travel together along the path to home.

AN EVOLVING STORY

Stories develop depth of character as they ripen and age. Heroes grow in both stature and aptitude as tales evolve, picking up from the end of one adventure to begin another. In story, the victorious adventurer Theseus, who slew the Minotaur, returned to Athens and ascended to the throne; his story continued. He became known as the "unifying king" for his achievement in creating political synergy by cooperatively uniting towns under one central governing power. The name "Theseus" is itself a joining together of two distinct English words: "these" followed by "us"; apart two separate groups, but together, one united hero through which another, perhaps stronger, chapter unfolds.

Our world is a cosmic maze of labyrinths; a place in which one may journey endlessly, meandering through a realm of thought-provoking possibilities, delighting in joyous exploration and discovery. Through action and inaction we find ourselves on an adventure, at times filled with glorious satisfaction, at times fraught with grave situations and dire consequences. To exist in a maze of labyrinths is to recognize that "Now" is our most amazing labyrinth; that mysterious, enigmatic puzzle of life's twists and turns...a bewildering state of complex confusion and ultimate reward.

The symbolic journey of the labyrinth is a place in which to seek one's center, not knowing when, or where, or if, we will face the threat of the Minotaur along our chosen path. The time it takes to enter the labyrinth, complete the adventure, and emerge through the point of entrance is unique to the pace set by each traveler. There are no wrong choices, no wrong turns. In a true labyrinth, continuing onward will lead to home…one entrance, one exit. Moving forward, trusting our inner strength, following the hero's clew laid before us long ago we complete the journey of one labyrinth, and upon our exit find that our world has somehow changed; our exit has become the entrance to another labyrinth. And so we are enticed to begin the next adventure, enter another labyrinth, another maze, all existing within a greater cosmic scheme of endless possibilities; a lifelong heroic journey of faith and determination.

Our lives abound, caught up in adventures in this universal, eternal maze of labyrinths. It would be wise to heed the lesson learned by those who have gone this way before. Maintain your grasp on the lifeline of the hero's clew as you thread your way along your chosen path, lest you succumb to the sound of your own voice echoing throughout the vast darkness and mistakenly follow it, like the beguiling call of an ancient Siren who sent would-be heroes crashing upon the rocks. Losing sight of the thread, isolated and alone, one could easily wander off into the sacrificial dining room of the Minotaur; quickly devoured and forgotten among the phantom trails and apparitions of those helpless victims who have gone before.

The metaphorical thread of the hero's clew is the unbreakable bond of our existence. It is the one thing we share which leads us safely through adventure to discover balance, and unified harmony. Joseph Campbell said that "the ancient myths were designed to harmonize the mind and body". Time may have faded their original intent, and meanings were washed away in the retelling. Some have been layered with the dust of ignorance until we no longer fully grasp their message. And yet we continue to tell the stories. It's as if by repeating them, their secrets will re-emerge like the entrance to the labyrinth reappeared as the hero's exit.

THE LABYRINTH WITHIN

Artistic design elements placed in a purposeful and distinct manner—whether through music, sculpting, or painting—produce an aesthetically pleasing and balanced integrated whole...a universal concept known as beauty. In life we seek harmony through emotional and physical balance; a natural state of equilibrium essential to our well-being. A constant reminder of this is carried in the signature of the labyrinth found within our own body.

The human ear; we draw attention to it by styling our hair to expose its outer surface and decorating its fleshy lobe with jewels. Within the passageway of the ear canal lies the middle ear, and deeper still, the inner ear. Parts of the outer, middle, and inner ear are designed to aid hearing; but the inner ear also helps maintain a sense of balance. The inner ear contains passages: one chamber called the "bony labyrinth", and a second chamber within the first called the "membranous labyrinth"—chambers named for their appearance—conjuring an image of the mythical lair of the Minotaur. The central area of the inner ear is the "vestibule", which connects the cochlea (a spiral-shaped cavity) to semi-circular canals aiding balance and equilibrium.

By definition a vestibule is an entrance, a portal, or threshold. One walks through the vestibule of a church to reach the patterned inlaid floor design of a labyrinth; a pilgrimage to spiritual balance, set in stone. The vestibule of our inner ear leads to an area of healthy bodily balance; our own intricate, divinely designed personal labyrinth. An inflammation in this area of the inner ear is called "labyrinthitis"; a discomfort characterized by nausea, dizziness, and problems with vision. (Perhaps similar symptoms were felt long ago as those Athenian youths drawn by lot were about to meet their dark fate with the Minotaur.)

Vertigo, a physical sensation of dizziness which can be caused by an abnormality in the inner ear, may be accompanied by symptoms of imbalance. The lesson of the labyrinth is not only carried in story, but is given to each of us in life: maintain healthy balance, and remain centered to complete the hero's journey.

LABYRINTHINE CHALLENGES

The labyrinth offers no escape to those chosen by lot. Once inside, there is no turning back…travel onward to complete the journey and reach the exit. A labyrinthine challenge may appear at any time. Nature thrusts her test upon us through the power of her design. The swirling pattern of a hurricane with its spiral form and distinctive center eye stares menacingly down at those in its path and tears into its mark with the fury of a raging beast. A strike from its outer bands is swift and harsh, yet its center, the eye, remains eerily calm. As with the double-edged axe the labyrinth of the hurricane cuts from both sides—once as it enters an area, and again as it leaves. Pre-warned of the approaching danger some choose to remain, only to be swallowed up in its path, while others flee to save the physical body, but return to a scene of material destruction and emotional devastation; challenged to rebuild or surrender.

✣═══ ═══✣

The spiral galaxy of the Milky Way, our home in the universe, was called "galaxias kyklos" or "milky circle" by the Greeks; the Romans described it as "via lactea", the "Milky Way". Viewed through the lens of a telescope, the Milky Way bears an uncanny resemblance to the swirling pattern of a hurricane; a labyrinth with a distinct center. Are we sacrificial prisoners trapped within a galactic labyrinth, or are we heroes re-living an adventurous journey—seeking, wandering, questing, discovering, remembering…for as long as the Fates allow?

+≈ ≈+

At times we impose our own challenges; testing our will. Routine or extraordinary, simple or complex, the steps we take and choices we make are designed to strengthen us. We subconsciously seek out the harmonizing pattern of the labyrinth in even the simplest daily tasks. Engaging in a workout at the gym, for example, is a quest to push ourselves to maintain a healthy balance between mind and body. There are days when our resolve is weak and our workout becomes the beast. Will we push ahead and rise to this heroic quest or throw in the towel and fall victim to failure and defeat?

Within the maze of the gym lies the dreaded labyrinth of the treadmill—one entrance, one exit; step on, walk, run, sweat, gasp for breath, and pray the time will quickly pass. Successfully fulfilling this self-imposed challenge we step off onto the same spot we entered, victorious in our goal; stronger, healthier, satisfied by the accomplishment. The completion of this latest battle is but a small victory and becomes no more than a passing memory as we go about our daily lives facing other challenges, other labyrinths; seeking balance and finding joy in peaceful, harmonious moments.

Life is entered and exited through the symbolic labyrinth of the womb...birthed from the biological mother and returned in burial within the sheltered tomb of Mother Earth. A reminder of this most sacred journey echoes in the words from the King James Bible, Genesis 3:19: "...till thou return unto the ground; for out of it wast thou taken: for dust thou art, and unto dust shalt thou return.". Our life experiences follow a course; be they through labyrinth or maze, cast upon us, or willingly chosen...we are the heroes.

We spin a yarn to tell a tale, a moral to the story; a lesson remembered and passed along the thread, one storyteller to the next. Layering strand upon strand we seek patterns of interlacing experiences, until we find that the story no longer exists apart from us but is absorbed into the essence of our very being, a shared belief, a remembered knowing that has always been. We are explorers, pioneers, and trailblazers; uncovering and interpreting clues, relying on hints, inklings, and gut instincts to guide us. Does life imitate story, or does story imitate life? The answer is, "Yes". Story was, is now, and will be. Life was, is now, and will be; until Atropos, the "Inevitable", cuts our thread.

CHAPTER FOUR

Artful Expression

Happy is he whom the Muses love...
~ Homer

To muse is to be absorbed in thought, to meditate or ponder. We are "amused" when our thoughts are pleasantly diverted, and left "bemused" when bewildered or confused. The "Mousai", the Muses, are Greek mythological deities given patronage over the arts. Known through the ancient poet Hesiod's *Theogony* as nine daughters of Zeus and Mnemosyne, each Muse oversees a particular ideal and is called upon for assistance in her specialty. These goddesses of remembered knowledge are: Clio, history; Calliope, epic poetry; Erato, romantic poetry; Euterpe, lyric poetry, Terpsichore, choral song and dance; Polyhymnia, sacred hymns; Urania, astronomy; Thalia, comedy; and Melpomene, tragedy. As deities of focused divine guidance, Muses have been personified throughout history and called forth as sources of inspiration.

REAL LIFE MUSES

"La gloriosa donna della mia mente" ("the glorious woman of my mind") is how the late 13th, early 14th century poet and writer Dante Alighieri described Beatrice, the real life muse said to have inspired his acclaimed works: *The Divine Comedy* and *La Vita Nuova*. Beatrice was a woman Dante met twice and had no physical relationship with. Yet, as a young woman she left such a deep, penetrating impression on him that her essence permeated his creations long after her death at a young age.

The composer Beethoven was said to have been inspired by the singer, Amalie Sebald. Perhaps it is she he addressed as his "Immortal Beloved" in personal letters found after his death. Impressionist artist Renoir was so taken with Aline Charigot, a model for many of his works, he married her. Pablo Picasso's relationship with the much younger Marie-Therese Walter produced a daughter, as well as inspiration for several of his works of art. One such piece believed to have been inspired by Marie-Therese is *Nude, Green Leaves and Bust*; created in 1932 and sold at auction in 2010 for over $100 million dollars…a fitting tribute to the divine favor of a Muse. Ancient museums were built as places of study and shrines to the Muses. Museums have kept their lore; becoming a gathering place to house, and reverently display, gloriously inspired collections of creative brilliance for all to behold.

LONGING TO COMMUNICATE

Creative inspiration takes form in countless ways: through speech and song, written symbols and pictures, dance and movement. What is meaningful to one may be nonsensical to another, and so we continually alter and adapt our manner to match the current mood, hoping to strike a harmonious chord of acceptance. We weigh responses and alter methods of delivery, choice of words, and mannerisms: softer, harsher, more humorous, more serious. Continually blending and adapting, we are driven to satisfy a primal need to communicate; to connect at a level which evokes acknowledgment, and inspires response.

We take on the role of the entertainer, an actor whose motivation is a yearning for acceptance. We hunger to be part of a greater experience, to convince ourselves and others that our message is worthy of being heard. In a scene from William Shakespeare's *As You Like It*, the character Jaques reminds us: "All the world's a stage, And all the men and women merely players; They have their exits and their entrances; And one man in his time plays many parts, acts being seven ages.".

From childhood on we are cast in a variety of roles, performing in improvised scenes of drama, comedy, and tragedy. Some hone their skills through formal training, others practice artful expression in more casual, playful environments.

Charades, for example, is an amusing game of communication played by both children and adult partygoers. The object of the game is to correctly decipher the message conveyed by a central figure; using means other than the spoken word. In Charades the actor begins by retrieving a concealed message written on a slip of paper. The actor launches into his performance by narrowing the subject matter for the audience, using previously learned and universally accepted gestures to identify categories: book, movie, song, quote.

A sense of urgency takes hold as the drama unfolds through a series of exaggerated facial expressions and bodily contortions; pointing, gesturing, and mimicking any number of theatrical moves to lead the audience to the correct interpretation of, what is in that moment, a message of utmost importance. With focused attention the participants eagerly await each clue cast forth; responding with wild guesses, anxiously hoping to be the first to crack the code. Stretching the imagination, testing boundaries, with laughter, and utterances of frustration, gameplay continues until someone yells out the correct answer…thereby affirming the successful and noteworthy performance of the actor in his latest starring role. While the audience revels in their triumphant discovery the pleased actor takes a seat and, in our moment of shared amusement, all are harmoniously content.

THEATER SYMBOLS

Charades draws inspiration from early theater. Speech and music were key elements in many Greek performances. Amplification through clever and skillful venue design greatly aided the audience in hearing sounds from the stage. But accomplished acting goes far beyond the spoken word; adding the complexity of nuanced impressions by setting the tone through body language, and subtle facial expression.

In large ancient theatrons (theaters), actors were staged a great distance from the furthest rows of the audience. Actors used dramatically exaggerated movements and gestures, colorful costumes and large masks depicting facial expressions as added assurance of delivering a more well-rounded and compelling story. Masks of sadness and tragedy were painted with painful and mournful expressions, while masks of comedy showed happy, smiling expressions. These contrasting dual facial characters, comedy and tragedy—the Muses, Thalia and Melpomene—are seen depicted in the familiar present day theater emblem.

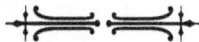

Actors are cued to take action and cued to prompt remembrance of their lines. Standing in a queue, we line up and await our cue to proceed to the performance viewing area; then weave our way as through the passageway of a labyrinth, following a route cordoned off by red ropes. In ancient Greece, citizens of Athens were all too familiar with the significance of red ropes; used as a means of crowd control. Citizens were rounded up and herded into political meetings of the Assembly by slaves stretching out a rope dipped in red dye. Those citizens who were slow to respond, or tried to resist the mandatory call for attendance, were marked by a stain from the rope's red dye. Easily identifiable through this branding, they were punished for their insubordinate action. Once the meetings were underway, the red-dyed rope was used to keep latecomers away, like we today block off places of no admittance using ropes and cords.

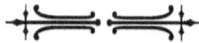

—<==⇒—

The mythic hero Theseus controlled his destiny by following a clew of thread laid down to show safe direction out of the labyrinth. A theater clew is the device which holds the weighted-line rigging that controls directed scenery changes on stage, methodically guiding actors through the story's settings from beginning to end. The audience's experience is enhanced by the sense of flow created as the changing scenery meshes with the performance of the actors. We sit back and enjoy the show until such time as cords are once again pulled to close the curtain; our cue to exit the theater, ever changed from this latest adventure. In theater, as in life, "knowing the ropes" is key.

"Orchestra" also makes its way through time. In Greek theaters of old the "orchestra" was the place for the "dancing chorus" of performers. In Roman theaters the "orchestra" was an area of reserved seating, from where dignitaries watched the staged performance. A modern-day theater "orchestra" is an ensemble of harmonious musical blending accompanying the actors' movements to enhance our enjoyment of the production. As vital elements, dance and music set the mood; at times themselves taking the lead role, stepping into the spotlight to become the story.

DANCE THROUGH LIFE OR FACE THE MUSIC

After Theseus slew the Minotaur, he fled with the other escaped Athenian youths to an isle on which they performed a dance of the labyrinth; retracing the adventure of his heroic steps, from entrance to center. Cultural dances often imitate versions of a hero's journey; setting in motion a story rooted in history, ritually played out in ceremony and handed down as tradition.

Choreography (from the Greek "khoreia"; dance) is a series of deliberate patterns and flowing movements arranged to convey a message, a story told through dance…from ballet to tango, hula to chorus line. Starring in our own story, we figuratively dance through life…sidestepping, spinning, and tiptoeing around, and through, issues. We dance to celebrate our joys and forget our sorrows, for religious ceremony, and to exercise our body. We Line, Square, Conga, Tap, and Waltz to our heart's content; dancing at public gatherings and in the privacy of our homes. We dance to lose ourselves in the moment, and we dance to remember who we are; to honor our ancestry and remind ourselves we are connected to someone or something greater.

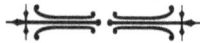

To "face the music" is accepting the consequences of our actions—a saying speculated to be rooted either in ancient theater, when stage performers stood at the mercy of their audience for praise or criticism; or taken from a ritual played out as disgraced military personnel were released from their ranks to the sound of a beating drum.

So goes the dance of life. As you face the music will you hear the exuberant welcoming call for an encore, or the solemn, shameful drumming out of defeat?

THE POWER OF SOUND

Music (art of the Muses) often accompanies dance. It is a universally understood form of expression resounding throughout the cosmos, with sounds floating around us, through us, and within us. Plucked from humanity's common thread, its inspiration and composition comes from all things…and no thing; sounds heard clearly, those silent to human ears yet heard by beasts, others merely sensed, echoing just beyond our reach. Our lives play out to the accompaniment of a sweeping symphony blended from nature, radiating down from the heavens, created through our daily routines, and present within our own bodies.

A rumble of thunder, tapping rain, and a howling wind cry out a warning for us to seek shelter. The melodious trill of a songbird, chirping crickets, the trickle of a stream cascading over stones bring thoughts of summer and a warm smile to our faces. The clatter of dishes (a familiar sound in the ritual of daily meal preparation) blends with periodic beeps, buzzes, and rings of electronic gadgets calling for our attention. The muffled ticking of our beating heart and the quiet undertone of our breathing keep time as comforting, repeating rhythms of life.

It was long believed the four humours (bodily fluids): blood, phlegm, yellow bile, and black bile were the keys to vitality. Ancient physicians theorized that good health occurred when these fluids were harmoniously balanced, and medical disorders and disease resulted from their imbalance. Pythagoras, 6th century BCE mathematician, scholar, and philosopher, was convinced that musical tones could influence one's health and temperament. By observing how music and rhythm affected one's senses and emotions he developed "musical medicine"—a therapeutic treatment for body and soul. Noting soothing music played to someone in an aggressive mood produced a calming effect, a variety of ills from melancholy (depression) to spasms were supplemented in treatment by using suggested melodies and tones.

Pythagoras established an exclusive school in Crotona, Italy wherein select initiates studied to learn his philosophy and master his teachings. At his school, songs were played in the morning to arouse the senses, clear the mind from sleep, and inspire creativity; in the evening songs were played to soothe, calm, and relax for a peaceful rest. Today we musically associate the energetic *Reveille* sounded by a bugle early in the morning as a call to rouse the troops, and the somber tones of *Taps* to signal day's end and slumber, or as a respectful final farewell at a funeral; remembrances of a distant yet familiar past.

Music as an instrument of healing has been studied and practiced through the ages, but it wasn't until the 20th century, through the work of E. Thayer Gaston (known as the "father of music therapy"), that music's role in healing was accepted as a viable discipline in the American health care system. Applied in a variety of treatments (to lower blood pressure, reduce anxiety and depression, manage pain levels, improve motor skills, and address behavioral issues), several universities now offer programs of study leading to professional designations and board certification in music therapy.

The mysterious power of music called the "Mozart Effect" (listening to the music of Mozart while in an awake or unconscious state) has been studied for a variety of reasons. A theory considered "controversial" by some, it has been demonstrated that listening to classical music can produce beneficial improvement in linguistic and spatial abilities (interpretation of visual perception), increased concentration, and enhanced ability to solve complex problems.

Therapists have found that in some patients whose speech had been impaired by stroke, improved response to relearning speech was aided through first singing or rhythmically chanting phrases to engage parts of the brain not normally associated with primary language and speech development.

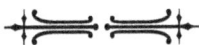

Depending on present mood (and personal taste), we may find music relaxing, distracting, joyful, sorrowful, calming, or irritating. By turning up the volume, or adding earphones to minimize external noises, we become immersed in the tones, awash with melodies which flow pleasantly through us; lost in momentary euphoria. Conversely, we quickly and frantically reach to turn down the volume, or search for earplugs to deaden any noisy, unpleasant tones; thereby stopping the resultant experience of a distressing sensation. The symptom of tinnitus (a ringing in the ears which can be caused by exposure to loud noise), may be accompanied by vertigo—a physical sensation of being off balance—calling forth the lesson of the labyrinth...remain centered.

Sound is more than bells and whistles, alarms and entertainment; it can be felt as well as heard. In a positive application, modern medicine uses its gentle sense in the ultrasound procedure, producing moving pictures generated by high-frequency sound waves. Some images provide a glimpse of developing life inside the body of a pregnant woman; others warn of impending danger, aiding in diagnostics and a course of treatment. Powerfully directed sound energy has been used to break up kidney stones into a size which can be flushed from the body.

But sound can also be a destructive force. In experimentation, it has been demonstrated that the human voice has the ability to shatter a drinking glass. Sound carries vibration; nature harnesses its force. All material matter has a natural resonant frequency; a speed at which, when reached, causes an object to vibrate. A violent vibration can produce catastrophic results. In 1940 the Tacoma Narrows Bridge (a suspension bridge in Washington State) was nicknamed "Galloping Gertie", describing its fierce swaying and undulating movement in the wind. Four months after it opened, the bridge shook itself into collapse. Technical experts hypothesized the bridge collapse was caused by resonance; the vibrational force produced by a human voice to shatter a glass.

Stories of sound's sheer power and command carry divine inspiration; dramatized in the story of Jericho. In the King James Bible, Joshua 6:4-5: "...seven priests shall bear before the ark seven trumpets of rams' horns: and the seventh day ye shall compass the city seven times, and the priests shall blow with the trumpets. And it shall come to pass, that when they make a long blast with the ram's horn, and when ye hear the sound of the trumpet, all people shall shout with a great shout; and the wall of the city shall fall down flat, and the people shall ascend up every man straight before him." And on that seventh day...the walls of Jericho came tumbling down.

During the Roman Empire, sound amplification played a vital role in the practical structure of architectural design. Amphitheaters in ancient cities could hold an audience of thousands, and were acoustically designed to carry sound throughout, from the closest to the furthest seats. Theatrons (theaters) embraced natural elements and were often skillfully built into hillsides, using surrounding rock as organic filter for sound waves, and wood for resonance.

Marcus Vitruvius Pollio (Vitruvius), the distinguished first century BCE Roman architect and engineer, painstakingly detailed precise building rules in his classic handbook, *De Architectura libi decem* (*The Ten Books on Architecture*).

Translations of his text are a mainstay reference for architects and engineers even today. Demonstrating his knowledge in building theaters, Vitruvius observed that ancient architects "followed in the footsteps of nature" to assure that voices from the stage ascended to the topmost rows of the audience by the application of harmonics. His principles on "symmetry in temples and the human body" were artistically expressed in Leonardo da Vinci's renowned 15th century drawing, "Vitruvian Man"—a study of anatomical proportions of the human body, named in honor of the great Roman architect, Vitruvius.

So compelling was a belief in the power of sound that in ancient times priests had special chambers constructed in which their spoken words or chants reverberated with great force to produce an awe-inspiring intonation. It was said that, over time, the wood and stone used to construct these sacred chambers became so imbued with these resounding vibrations that when the structure itself was struck, it released imbedded tones to reproduce at will.

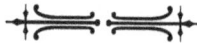

Many centuries later words spoken by the renowned twentieth century architect Frank Lloyd Wright echo in our minds with ties to this ancient past. Wright said: "Whether people are fully conscious of this or not, they actually derive countenance and sustenance from the 'atmosphere' of the many things they live in or with. They are rooted in them just as a plant is in the soil in which it is planted." Believing that buildings should "grow naturally from their surroundings" Wright's designs harmoniously blended with nature.

Architecture, filled with energy and spirit, is experienced through the perception and feel of its lively design. Each painstakingly crafted pattern resounds with the blended accompaniment of each individual who collaborated on its creation. "Architecture is like frozen music" is a beautifully expressed sentiment attributed to Johann Wolfgang von Goethe, the late 18th, early 19th century German writer and philosopher.

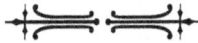

Where do sounds "go" once they've been created? Perhaps, as with ancient sound chambers, they are absorbed as energy into every thing…and no thing. Could the controlled force of amplified sound vibration—resonance—be harnessed and directed on a large enough scale to deliver constructive as well as destructive power; perhaps used in elevating and moving objects with as much ease as it shatters, dissolves, and destroys?

Were the gigantic stones and building materials used in creation of the wonders of the ancient world guided into placement by a sophisticated knowledge of directed sound energy, that has long since been forgotten? If such knowledge existed once upon a time, or long ago and far away, it exists today, lying dormant, waiting to be remembered back into being.

LYRE AND HARP

In the *Homeric Hymn to Hermes* the young god crafted a wondrous musical lyre (harp) from a mountain tortoise's shell stretched with seven strings of sheep gut, and presented it as a gift to Apollo. Apollo mastered the instrument's melodious tones and became the musical director of the heavenly voices known as the Choir of the Muses. Calliope, Muse of epic poetry, bore a son, Orpheus, who displayed such musical aptitude Apollo gave to him this extraordinary lyre. Orpheus's remarkable musical ability was unsurpassed by god or mortal. So alluringly did he play that all of nature gave pause to listen while he soothed the savage beast, moved rocks, and uprooted trees with his song.

Orpheus used the power of music to lull into a trance Cerberus, the three-headed guard dog at the entrance of the Underworld; allowing Orpheus to safely enter in search of his beloved wife, Eurydice, who had died from a serpent's poisonous bite shortly after their wedding. Upon her death Eurydice (as were all departed souls) was escorted to the Underworld to spend eternity; but Orpheus pursued his beloved, determined to bring her back.

Hades, Lord of the Underworld, was deeply touched by the sound of this beautiful music, and allowed Eurydice to follow Orpheus out of the Underworld...with this warning...Orpheus was not to look back at her until they emerged into the land of the living. As they made their way up the passageway Orpheus could bear no longer to wonder if Eurydice was indeed behind him. Disregarding Hades's warning, Orpheus turned backed to glance at his beloved; and as he did, she was snatched back into the Underworld.

Orpheus joined the hero Jason on his famed voyage in quest of the Golden Fleece. It was Orpheus's music that charmed the Argonauts and saved them from being lured to certain death at sea by the beguiling call of the Sirens.

Alas, poor Orpheus met his fate, dying a horrid death; his body torn apart at the hands of the Ciconian Maenads—the raging mad women. His head they separated from its body, then cast his parts into the river along with his lyre. As his severed head and the musical lyre floated along, they attached and fused together as one.

Long ago the lyre was viewed as a symbol of human embodiment. The body of the lyre represented the physical form, its strings the nerves, and the musician who played it the spirit. In life our actions "strike a chord" or "hit a nerve", symbolically plucking the lyre's strings to spark an emotional response; the former more pleasant than the latter.

The lyre was personified as a talking harp in the tale of *Jack and the Beanstalk.* The Giant who stole the harp from the knight called it a "faithful servant". The Giant commanded the harp to play and it played a sad tune. He commanded it to play something merrier, and it obeyed. And when he commanded it to play a lullaby the harp played so sweetly the Giant fell asleep. Jack waited for the Giant to nod off, then swooped in, seized the talking harp, and made off with it.

To "harp" on something means to dwell incessantly or annoyingly. In Greek mythology the Harpies fulfilled this role as winged creatures said to be personified gusts of wind…"snatchers" who would swoop down and fly off with objects or people. In myth, the Harpies were sent to torment the blinded King Phineas. They repeatedly stole food set out for him; a punishment dealt by Zeus for the king's misuse of his gift of prophecy. It was the brave Argonauts who drove away the Harpies and saved King Phineas from his torturous fate.

In modern-day homes "harp" takes on a mundane task. It is the curved metal frame bent around a lightbulb (symbol for an idea or thought) to hold a lampshade in place. In death, Orpheus's head (thought) attached itself to his musical lyre (harp)…a symbolic representation carried inside our own head.

The limbic system of the human brain functions as a control center that interprets emotional, motivational, and behavioral responses related to survival instincts (fear, anger, pleasure), and regulates automatic functions (sleep cycles, appetite, body temperature). The limbic system also plays an important role in memory...determining which memories are stored, where in the brain they are stored, and retrieving them when necessary.

Between the brain's hypothalamus (emotions) and hippocampus (memory) is the fornix—an arching band of nerve fibers, where signals pass through. These fibers are referred to as the "lyra", named for their shape that bears a physical resemblance to the musical lyre. This lyra (harp) bridges memory and emotion sectors in the brain. In myth Orpheus played his musical lyre to evoke deep emotional response (hypothalamus). His grandmother was Mnemosyne, goddess of memory and remembrance (hippocampus) and mother of the inspirational Muses.

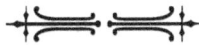

As each unique form of expression makes its way into the world, it harmonizes...or clashes...with the whole. Whether you take inspiration from an outward source, or hail your inner Muse through quiet meditation, once the connection is called forth we contemplate and ruminate until...as the brilliant scientist Archimedes was said to have exclaimed...

"Eureka!"(I have found it!), and we are inspired to create yet another glorious masterpiece. To call forth the Muses has been the way for thousands of years. As Hesiod explains in *Theogony*, it is "The Mousai (Muses) who gladden the great spirit of their father Zeus in Olympos with their songs, telling of things that are and that shall be and that were aforetime with consenting voice."

CHAPTER FIVE

WHAT YOU MYTH IS WHAT YOU GET

*When we try to pick out anything by itself,
we find it is tied to everything else in the universe*
~ John Muir

S tories are the messengers of time; legacies spun through the ages. Myths blend deep-rooted themes with cultur- ally entrenched insights as they travel along an unbroken stream of consciousness. Early cultures handed down me- ticulously crafted and richly laden tales with the same care as we pass along precious heirlooms; cherished memories of times before. Encased within each heirloom rest the stories of all whose lives were touched as the treasure passed among and between generations, capturing history in the making.

Echoes of expressive life-patterning tales are cloaked in metaphor to soften a harsh truth and disclose a hidden danger;

to bore their way to the depth of universal understanding. A savvy observer, well aware of the powerful structure and form of the rhythmic verse, notes the finer details and uncovers clues wrapped within the delivery. Beneath the wrapping lies the true reward. Bits and pieces of the deeper meaning are gathered up, then folded back into the mix; producing a richer overall experience.

Be forewarned…each storied treasure, however radiant or enticing, has its imperfections. The key is to recognize whether what we see is of pure and genuine form, or merely a sly deception—fool's gold passed among us as a misguided belief. A flaw compromises value only to those whose keen eye is able to discern its existence and assess its impact on the whole. Whether or not the flaw adds character and distinction, or weakens and cheapens the whole, lies in perception—our ability to intuitively "grasp with the mind" and satisfy within ourselves the meaning of "worth". Each of us defines "value" in our own way.

Ancient myths are such treasures; requiring careful scrutiny before accepting or spreading an effectual interpretation. Significant, perhaps life-altering, meanings may be uncovered within the storied deeds and symbols of ancient gods; but look closely and choose wisely before tipping the scale of intent to favor one view over another. The spaces between the words give pause to reflect on a deeper meaning, silently guiding conclusions into place. A shiny new tale may temporarily blind us from seeing the truth behind the cunning slight of hand. When the distraction of the outer polish is worn away by the winds of time, even the most obscure flaw is exposed. And those aligned with its illusion are weakened in kind.

MYTH OF THE CADUCEUS

The symbol of the caduceus is an emblem many today associate, through common usage, with the medical profession. Shown as a staff entwined by two snakes along its shaft and a pair of spreading wings at its top, we take comfort in its display; entrusting our most precious asset—healthful well-being—to those who practice under its representation. But stories of the caduceus reveal complexities more entwined than the snakes it carries. Illusion or truth? Unravel the tale of Hermes, Greek messenger of the gods: overseer of merchants and commerce, liars and thieves, travelers, communication and mediation; son of Zeus and the nymph Maia, to search for clues.

In his role as psychopomp Hermes guided departed souls on their journey into the afterlife; himself traveling freely between the world of the living and the Underworld of the dead. He is the shapeshifter, the trickster associated with the wily coyote, the essence of the clever, cunning, loveable scoundrel in every tale. The *Homeric Hymn to Hermes* tells of the god Hermes as the baby who crept from his crib, and by darkness stole cattle from his brother Apollo's prized herd. He cleverly disguised his footprints, strapping boughs of trees to the bottom of his feet, then drove Apollo's cattle to a meadow, sacrificed two, and contentedly wandered home.

Apollo, possessing the gift of prophecy, suspected his trickster half-brother of this thieving act and brought a complaint against Hermes to their father, Zeus. The silver-tongued Hermes professed his innocence, claiming no part in this abhorred crime for which he was accused. Zeus, while amused by such clever antics, was not fooled by Hermes's portrayal of innocence and commanded that he return to Apollo that which was rightfully his.

So impressed was Zeus with Hermes's gift of eloquent and persuasive speech he appointed him messenger of the gods, and bestowed upon him a wand called the caduceus— a herald's staff bearing wings. Hermes, as mediator, was said to have encountered two snakes at odds on a road. Thrusting down his herald's wand between them he bade them resolve their differences; whereupon the two snakes coiled together along the staff of Hermes's caduceus, forever entwined upon it as a symbolic reminder of cooperation and accord.

THE BUSINESS OF HERMES AND MERCURY

Hermes's patronage over commerce and communication continue in present day. The god's Roman counterpart is Mercury (from the Latin "merx" merchandise), with whom the planet shares its name. Both gods are frequently depicted in artistic renderings carrying a caduceus and wearing winged footwear and headgear.

In modern usage, the mythological role of Mercury as swift messenger and overseer of commerce is easily recognizable in the FTD logo. As storytellers, FTD embraced the essence of this iconic symbol but adapted it to better align with their own message—replacing the caduceus wand Mercury carried in myth with a more suitable symbol—a bouquet of flowers.

Adorned with FTD's modern embellishment Mercury (Hermes) continues to fulfill his ancient patronage. He oversees communication of orders, purchase of merchandise, attachment of personal notes; then safely guides their speedy delivery. They further capture the essence of mythic symbolism with the "Mercury Network" (an electronic system used throughout the floriculture industry to process orders and messages), also known as the "Floral Information Superhighway".

Symbols flashed before our eyes burn their way to the heart of a deeper connection. Searching for an inkling of remembrance from times before and those to come they rest on ideas which resonate with the present moment; focusing a spotlight on lasting and powerfully convincing messages. Our choices: accept what is, modify, or replace. Yet regardless of the action, or how much time passes, the shadow of that which has already been cannot be obliterated; a footprint, a soft echo, however faint, remains forever impressed upon the essence of humankind.

Choices span generations and blend a myriad of ideas… remembrances old and new; filtered, shaded, adapted to form "other" truths—ones not necessarily better, but perhaps more befitting the moment. At times these newly formed composites mix or distort the meaning and purpose of the original message in such a way that the new whole appears unequal to the sum of its parts; the emergence of another symbol's power has been summoned forth.

THE ROD OF ASCLEPIUS

For thousands of years the Rod of Asclepius, a physician's staff of distinction and authority, stood in the world as the time-honored emblem to signify the healing arts. Differing from the caduceus wand of Hermes, the Rod of Asclepius bears no wings; its long, simple staff is coiled by a single serpent in recognition of the widespread use of snakes in ancient healing rites; shedding their skin seen as a symbol of rebirth and renewal.

In Greek mythology Asclepius, son of the god Apollo and the mortal woman Coronis, was taught the healing arts by the Centaur Chiron. Asclepius's skills evolved until as a highly gifted healer he practiced beyond human aptitude; experimenting with the blood of a Gorgon (Medusa creature). Myth holds that blood drawn from the left side of a Gorgon acts as a deadly poison, but blood from the right side of a Gorgon holds power to resurrect the dead. Asclepius, reaching beyond mortal healing limits, was upsetting the natural order; playing God to change the course of life, choosing who would live or die, taking money in exchange for his gift of restoring life. Enraged by these bold actions Zeus cast down a mighty thunderbolt and struck Asclepius dead.

Despite briefly succumbing to the seductive power of his godlike abilities Asclepius had served humankind well, and for his honorable deeds he is immortalized. His physician's staff—the Rod of Asclepius—has been a widely accepted emblem displayed by medical professionals since ancient times. His gift of healing continues through his children: Hygeia offers hygiene, cleanliness and the preservation of health; and Panaceia, the all-healing, gives the cure-all remedy for disease (panacea).

ADAPTATION VS MISINTERPRETATION

Meaningful stories adapt to fit the times. Maintaining cultural significance relies on the storyteller to honor and convey the essence of the original underlying message. Like fire given fuel travels swiftly on the wind, under the right conditions manipulation and distortion, or innocent misinterpretation and heartfelt assertions are passed along as fact. These sparks quickly burn their way into our psyches; spreading wildly as beliefs, engulfing an ideal until all that remains of the original is its scorched outline. Early 20th century America fell under one such illusion when a smoldering change in symbolic representation combusted into a raging inferno, its flames fanned by the breath of commerce.

Confusion and distrust weighed heavily on the minds of Americans during this period. A desperate need to regain economic health and well-being, and mitigate widespread greed and alleged corruption in business was evident. The late 19th and early 20th centuries were known as the "Progressive Era", a time when many favored government regulation over business. The Interstate Commerce Act (1887) and the Sherman Antitrust Act (1890) were enacted; conditions were right to set the spark ablaze.

In 1902 the caduceus wand carried by the messenger god Hermes was chosen by the U.S. Army Medical Corps as its emblem; sending a ripple through time, mixed messages and crossed purpose as commerce (Hermes's wand) mingled with the healing arts (Rod of Asclepius). The powerful significance of the Rod of Asclepius was weakened, as if Zeus himself cast down a mighty thunderbolt.

Did the collective pain from a country's need to produce a healthier economy overwhelm sacred symbology and produce a distorted illusion of the Rod of Asclepius? Perhaps the image blurred and was misconstrued as a rendering of a dollar sign—a single snake, symbol of rebirth and renewal, coiled in the shape of the letter "S" around a straight shaft; its once singular purpose giving way to a clash of ideals.

In myth, patronage was at times shared or transferred between the gods; a storyteller favoring one version over another without explanation. A new version of a nation's story began when Hermes (commerce) stepped in where Asclepius (healing) had ruled. Patronage over modern-day healing arts began to shift away from Asclepius toward Hermes.

HERALDING THE ARRIVAL OF HERMES

The Institute of Heraldry, a department whose charge it is to "take responsibility for the coordination and approval of coats of arms and other insignia", for all branches of the federal government, offers the following explanation on their web site. "Rooted in mythology, the caduceus, historically an emblem of physicians symbolizes knowledge, wisdom, promptness, and various aspects of medical skill." Not surprisingly, the Institute of Heraldry falls under the patronage of Hermes as the official messenger and herald of the gods.

Such a convincing, cleverly-worded message delivered by an authoritative body is meant to reassure us; but carries the underlying tone of the trickster himself. "Historically an emblem of physicians", they say. Perhaps there is more to their story…some truth hidden from us; for attempts to link this symbol to western medicine produced but a few obscure references.

The 16th century publisher Frobenius (Froben) used a form of the caduceus, without spreading wings but with a sitting bird (dove) atop the staff, as his printer's mark in medical publications. A similar caduceus-like symbol was displayed in the personal coat of arms for Sir William Butts, 16th century court physician to King Henry VIII. The coat of arms for John Caius, another prominent physician of the 16th century and founder of Caius College in Cambridge, is said to have displayed a herald's wand to signify prudence or wisdom. And the coat of arms for William Harvey (17th century physician to kings James I and Charles I), acknowledged for his discoveries in the circulation of blood, displayed a caduceus-like emblem without wings.

The word "caduceus" is rooted in the Greek "karykeion", meaning "herald's staff", a clear tie to the messenger god. As history demonstrates, the beliefs of a few can quickly spread, infect the masses, and engulf all that has gone before. Curiously, acceptance of this new story—heralding Hermes's caduceus as a medical symbol—has been primarily contained within pockets of the United States. In stark contrast to the Hermes caduceus insignia selected by the

U.S. Army Medical Corps, the prestigious American Medical Association adopted the more universally accepted symbol, the the Rod of Asclepius, for use in their emblem; as did the World Health Organization, the British Medical Association, the Royal Army Medical Corps, the Canadian Medical Association, and countless other esteemed worldwide medical organizations. The Star of Life emblem, commonly seen and prominently displayed on medical emergency vehicles in the United States, also bears the insignia of the Rod of Ascelpius.

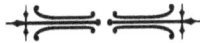

Confusion surrounded emblem choices in two branches of medicine in the United States; with both ultimately displaying a form of the Rod of Asclepius. In 1965 the American Dental Association adopted the Rod of Asclepius placed within the Greek letters Delta (Δ) and Omicron (O) as the official emblem of dentistry, yet it is still called a "caduceus" on their web site; perhaps a subconscious nod to Hermes's influence—using "mercury" in dental fillings was a common practice.

In 1970 the American Veterinary Association adopted the Rod of Asclepius overlaid by a large letter "V" as their insignia; replacing a previously used style of Hermes's caduceus. The veterinary branch of medicine has long practiced euthanasia, a representation of Hermes in his role as psychopomp who guided departed souls into the Underworld. Past use of the caduceus emblem acknowledged the significance of those practitioners appointed to fulfill the role of modern day guides for our beloved pets, who journey into the afterlife when "put to sleep".

A shadow was cast over the rich history of the Rod of Asclepius as more and more medical professionals aligned with Hermes's caduceus wand; energized by mass media marketing campaigns. In a matter of decades, thousands of years of folklore, home remedies, and house calls were propelled into commercial medicine and big business. Whether the U.S. Army Medical Corps was influenced in their choice of Hermes's caduceus through a misinterpretation of myth or simply considered it a more artistically appealing insignia, as the chosen symbol its expanded role in our culture has struck a chord, awakening a subconscious need to redefine our own "medical myth"; a shift toward a new and evolving story.

Weighing one symbol against the other tips the balance in favor of commerce as Hermes's caduceus becomes more and more widely displayed; a culture willingly—or unknowingly—aligns with its mythic call. Some artistic renderings cleverly morph the two snakes on Hermes's caduceus into a DNA strand; perhaps a more plausible medical association in our minds.

Rising health care costs and slashed medical benefits shift emphasis from patient well-being to a "healthy bottom line".

A deluge of commercial advertising moves us from the role of patient to customer under Hermes's influence; opening the door for widespread change.

A TIME OF CHANGE

Feeling the power of his newly-bestowed medical patronage Hermes took aim at another longstanding tradition. The shapeshifter oversaw replacement of the classical version of the Hippocratic Oath (a pledge of ethics recited by many medical students who swear to abide by its tenets). As a longstanding tradition, the classical Hippocratic Oath (named in honor of Hippocrates, 5th century BCE "father of western medicine") was widely accepted. Then in 1964, Louis Lasagna, Academic Dean of the School of Medicine at Tufts University composed a radically modified Hippocratic Oath, one which displaced the classical.

In the classical version, the oath taker swears by the ancient gods and goddesses to fulfill said covenant. The classical version openly states that a deadly drug will not be given to anyone who asks for it, nor will the physician suggest such to the patient. And it makes clear that no woman will be given an abortive remedy.

The modern version forgoes the ancient deities, paying homage to science and those physicians who have gone before. The modern iteration inserts the option "it may also be within my power to take a life". Through its very terminology the 1964 reinterpretation may have subconsciously opened a door to both legalized abortion and assisted suicide (euthanasia).

Befitting the times, the 1964 American version of the Oath drastically altered the classical version during a period of economic expansion, civil rights, radical change, and counterculture revolution. Some have mockingly nicknamed this modern version the "Hypocritical Oath"; noting that its wording shifts focus away from patient to emphasize powers bestowed upon doctor. The Hippocratic Oath, that oft recited code of ethics, represented a longstanding humble reminder to all who pledged their devotion to the noble and respected nature of medicine. We, a new generation of storytellers, adapted and redistributed patronage among the gods, freely interpreting and embellishing myths to suit the moment; a fragment of our medical culture changed by the power of words.

THE POWER OF WORDS

Words carry energy. Strung together in deliberate fashion, spoken with conviction, and delivered with great passion they wield enough power to spur us to action. "The tongue is mightier than the blade" is an expression attributed to Euripedes, 5th century BCE. Its sentiment echoes through time, appearing as Shakespeare's familiar literary line: "The pen is mightier than the sword" from *Hamlet*; and again rephrased by Thomas Jefferson in a 1792 letter to Thomas Paine as: "Go on then in doing with your pen what in other times was done with the sword: shew that reformation is more practicable by operating on the mind than on the body of man…".

Time and again inspiration is sparked as the penetrating words of a charismatic speaker resound. "Let us not seek to satisfy our thirst for freedom by drinking from the cup of bitterness and hatred…I have a dream…", said Martin Luther King, Jr. in his impassioned speech delivered from the steps of the Lincoln Memorial. John F. Kennedy empowered a nation with words spoken during his Inaugural Address: "…ask not what your country can do for you—ask what you can do for your country.". And Neil Armstrong's memorable words from that historic first moment on the moon: "That's one small step for man; one giant leap for mankind.", opened a door to a wondrous new frontier of exploration for an entire world.

READING BETWEEN THE LINES

Each letter of the alphabet is a symbol. Alone, a letter carries limited meaning. Vowels strategically placed within consonants form familiar patterns…words. Words strung together in deliberate sequence communicate tone-setting phrases. By reading not only the lines themselves, but also "reading between the lines", our minds formulate an overall sense of what is being conveyed; something felt on a much deeper level. An insult is hurtful; we cower under the severe reprimand of a "tongue-lashing", feeling the sharpness of each word as it pierces our psyche. In contrast, when paid a glowing compliment we radiate and smile.

Powerful words, whether positive or negative, carry such force that the message is both heard in the mind and felt in the body. To "shrink from embarrassment" and "swell with pride" conjure pictures from a scene in *Alice's Adventures in Wonderland* as she drank from the bottle and shrunk to a mere 10 inches in size, then ate the little cake and grew to nine feet tall.

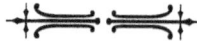

The modern version of the Hippocratic Oath blends two myths: Hermes the psychopomp who escorts souls to the Underworld, and Asclepius the healer reaching beyond mortal medicine, choosing who would live or die. A warning is clear in this new Oath: "Most especially must I tread with care in matters of life and death.". Justice weighs in when this fine line is crossed; a modern day prison sentence replaces the lightning bolt cast down by Zeus. Caution travels through time, from an ancient Oath to its modern-day rewrite, making an appearance through Shakespeare's titled character Hamlet as he reflects on death in his famous monologue: "To be, or not to be, that is the question...to die, to sleep...must give us pause.".

With history as our witness we bow to Hermes's gift of persuasive communication and feel the energetic power of words and the effective use of symbols as catalysts for action. Favoring the emblem of Hermes's caduceus over the time-honored Rod of Asclepius, and rewriting the words to a revered Oath were two changes of mythical proportion that left their marks on present day. Hermes swiftly delivered the message that reform hangs in the balance as medicine aligns with myth. Discontent with the current health care system in the United States (business overshadowing the humanitarian objective) brings great discomfort and widespread (dis)ease.

Could establishing a universally accepted medical symbol and crafting a more balanced Oath (recognize scientific advances yet still honor classical history) bridge the gap between commerce and health? Perhaps the trickster Hermes has intentionally instilled confusion as a clever ruse; delivering a message that both emblems have their place in medical culture and we are left to sort it out. Perhaps the Rod of Asclepius is best attuned to symbolize professional medical practitioners and caregivers who honor the long rich history of ancient healers; while commercial medical ventures (medical supplies, advertising) are more in alignment with

Hermes's symbol of commerce; a clear distinction between patient and customer.

Aftermath follows change; the challenge lies in reasonably predicting whether the results will be perceived as adding to or taking away from the overall well-being. We must be prepared to accept repercussions, and be willing to make adjustments to achieve the intended goal; ever conscious of consequences. Hermes, the shapeshifter masking his footprints, the trickster using clever slight of hand to impart his shrewd sense of commerce into the mix, is all too eager to assist; causing turmoil to get our attention if need be.

THE GUISE OF THE TRICKSTER

Hesiod identifies Hermes as the one who bestowed upon Pandora (her name meaning "all-gifted") a "shameless mind and deceitful nature", and instructed her not to open her "jar" (later known as a "box"). Did Hermes offer Pandora sincere wise counsel, or was it his intent to use reverse psychology and trick her into opening her jar, releasing ills into the world? By the same token, was selecting Hermes's caduceus to symbolize the noble healing arts the ultimate medical misdiagnosis...an egregious mistake...or was it a cleverly designed catalyst stemming from within our collective unconscious, perfectly timed, calling forth the cunning messenger to direct our attention to an outdated health care system in dire need of reform? Perhaps there are greater powers at work.

We sit spellbound, besieged by commercial ads, urged to take "this little pill" or "that supplement"; cheerfully offered a list of purported benefits, followed by a more subdued litany of potentially serious side effects quickly rattled off by a silver-tongued narrator (Hermes). Like a scene from Lewis Carroll's *Alice's Adventures in Wonderland*, upon finding a bottle labeled "DRINK ME" and a cake marked "EAT ME" we cling to a promised outcome and succumb to hope; dismissing the potential risks as long as it is not marked "poison". For as Alice warns us: "...if you drink much from a bottle marked 'poison', it is almost certain to disagree with you, sooner or later.".

Blind faith may very well lead us headlong down a rabbit hole, falling into some strange illusion of a medical Wonderland—a place where the Cheshire Cat told Alice: "...we're all mad here. I'm mad. You're mad." "How do you know I'm mad?", said Alice. "You must be...or you wouldn't have come here." And in true form the body of the Cheshire Cat vanished, leaving behind an enormous grin which remained for some time. To borrow a phrase from Alice, how very "curiouser and curiouser" our lives have become. Like Alice, in the end, we must awaken from our dreamlike state to escape this Wonderland, or it will surely lead us all into madness.

THE PERILS OF MERCURY

Used in a variety of applications from scientific instruments to streetlights and advertising signs, "quicksilver", another name for the metallic element mercury, translates from the Latin "argentum vivum" as "living silver". In its liquid state it fills barometers and thermometers, serving as a helpful guide and indicator of change from the norm; visibly traveling up and down a sealed tube.

Ironically, overexposure to the element mercury poisons us, sending us to seek treatment from those very medical professionals who may have chosen to practice under the caduceus symbol of Mercury (Hermes)…those who use a thermometer filled with mercury to determine our state of health. Absorbed into the fish we eat, mercury can come from waters tainted with industrial processing materials; perhaps those very pharmaceuticals we might well ingest in prescribed dosages at other times to aid us in recovery from sickness.

"Mad as a hatter" is a 19th century phrase used long before Lewis Carroll's *Alice's Adventures in Wonderland* was published. The phrase described an occupational disorder affecting the nervous system; a condition believed caused by exposure to prolonged contact with the element mercury used in the manufacture of hats during this period. Lewis Carroll named his character, "Hatter"; it was the grinning Cheshire Cat in the story who described Hatter, and other characters, as "mad". Later versions of the story adopted this description as part of the name and the character was henceforth known as "Mad Hatter".

Exposure to mercury, long believed to pose a health risk, is a high profile environmental safety concern. In 2005, the European Union (EU) launched the "mercury strategy", a comprehensive plan to globally address mercury pollution. The EU plan outlined measures to reduce mercury emissions, cut supply and demand, and protect against exposure and contamination in fish. Progress has been made through restrictions on sale of devices containing mercury, a ban on exports of mercury from the EU, and new rules on safe storage.

Mercury combined with other metals forms an amalgam which was, until recently, used to fill the cavities in our teeth. Chewing on these packed bits of mercury serves as a reminder that Hermes, overseer of communication— the silver-tongued trickster—may be putting words in our mouths. In recent decades there has been a conscious movement away from using mercury as a dental filling; perhaps we have become wise to this clever trickster.

THAT'S ENTERTAINMENT

Hermes, whose patronage extends over many areas of our lives, loves an audience. He easily crosses from real life drama into the world of entertainment to influence our thoughts on well-being by carving inroads into the big business of medically-themed television: sitcoms, dramas, and reality-based informational programs with real life doctors in the starring roles. Fast-paced snippets of medical advice are rattled off to pack the hour, or half hour; set among strategically well-placed commercial breaks. Actors learn key medical terminology and phrases to impress upon us the possibility that the scenario being portrayed could very well happen in real life. As we travel with Hermes between the worlds of reality and fantasy, for a brief moment, we are tricked into believing the illusion.

However myth makes its way into the world—in grand fashion or in subtle and intriguing ways—it brings with it possibilities and opportunities for great change, influencing our lives befitting the times. Hermes makes his swift entrance, taking on a role, a persona of his choosing from the many he, as shapeshifter, has mastered. Whether we meet him in the guise of the trickster, merchant, liar, mediator, herald, psychopomp; or wrapped in yet another of the many cloaks this loveable scoundrel wears, rest assured, we will feel his influence many times.

CHAPTER SIX

As Above, So Below

Somewhere, something incredible is waiting to be known
~ Carl Sagan

Long before modern day distractions, before our lives became "simplified" by a multitude of techno-gadgets, before light pollution poured forth from cities and dulled our view, before we relied on external media to interpret and prioritize our thinking there was a desire to understand the world through contemplation, imagination, and active participation. Under the watchful eye of Urania, Muse of Astronomy, humankind looked with inspirational reverie at the grand allure of the sky; searching for a key to unlock its mysterious messages.

Humankind continues to search the heavens for answers. Those who gaze upon the universe through the lens of the heart are offered a glimpse into its divine soul. A night sky is filled with twinkling lights, and floating, glowing orbs set against a vast backdrop of darkness. Rich splashes of color brush across an early morning sky. The welcoming rays of first daylight give way to blinding midday sun, then another show of color at day's end. Suspended masses of puffy clouds are set in motion, and wisp into imaginative shapes overlaid on a canopy of blue and gray. Resplendent in her glory, this magnificent universe shares her spectacle without prejudice. All of humankind: servant or royal, man, woman, or child may freely observe the wonder of the heavens and share in her many moods.

LETTERHEAD OF THE GODS

Before us exists a universe beckoning to be noticed, biding its time, patiently waiting for us to understand and develop; like a parent observes its child learn to speak, then read and write, and evolve into a unique being who takes part in the creation of a profound masterpiece. The universe speaks in authoritative tones: gentle raindrops, loud claps of thunder, soothing cool breezes, harsh bitter cold; shattering communication barriers to transcend humankind's perceived limitations and rigid beliefs.

To understand its messages we must do more than cast a cursory glance skyward; we must learn to see deeper through thoughtful contemplation...we must muse. Sky is the letterhead of the gods, filled with celestial calligraphy written in a language known to poets, songwriters, artists, and storytellers; waiting to be studied and translated by earthly dreamers, scholars, and scribes.

A daunting task was set before the ancients...to unlock the writings. The heavens appear boundless; how then to study its script without becoming overwhelmed by the sheer size of the stationery on which the flowing messages appeared? Celestial bodies travel at various speeds, some move independently of one another yet seem connected. Like characters in a story, each fulfills a role. Surely the mythic gods meant for this glorious choreographic display as more than entertainment. Perhaps it was sage advice offered from profoundly divine thinkers. The ancients set out to study, interpret, and record celestial observations to determine beneficial significance and application to daily life. But where to begin?

Without instruction or guidance, a sense of overwhelming frustration befalls a novice star gazer trying to pinpoint the location of a particular planet, star, or constellation. Where should one focus their line of sight? Imagine if you happened upon an enormous open field on which countless ball games were being simultaneously played—a field stretching in all directions as far as the eye can see. With no discernible outer boundaries, and thousands of players of all shapes and sizes in similar dress moving against a backdrop of green grass, how would you, the spectator, distinguish one game from the next? Who are the players, the coaches, the referees...the other spectators? What is the object of each game? What are the rules? Which teams are being eliminated and which are winning...and what is the reward or punishment that comes with winning or losing?

Ancient scholars devised a system through which to independently observe, record, and decipher data; then added individual findings into collective compilations to develop a broader meaningful reference. Assumptions and plausible conclusions were drawn by identifying correlations between the movement of celestial bodies above and events unfolding on Earth. Generation after generation contributed data to produce the sum of the whole; revising, layering, and enriching the foundation with each new discovery.

Early Babylonian astronomer-priests were credited with the development of a "system of celestial omens"—called the seed of modern Western astrology. This new discipline, a protoscience, was the social science of its time; cultivated within the fertile minds and under the watchful eyes of the most trusted, learned, and reverent members of a group. Astrology, derived from the ancient Greek "astron" (star) and "logos" (speech), evolved as a tool used to interpret the symbolic messages displayed by the celestial bodies.

THE CLASSICAL PLANETS

Five planets: Mercury, Venus, Mars, Jupiter, and Saturn were known to the ancients as the "wandering stars". These five, along with the two luminaries, Sun and Moon, are called the "classical planets". These celestial bodies could be seen with the naked eye and appeared to move independently of one another, making them distinguishable from the immense body of countless "fixed stars" which seemed to move together in a synchronized dance across the stage of the sky.

The classical planets were ascribed to seven sacred vowels: Alpha, Epsilon, Eta, Iota, Omicron, Upsilon, and Omega; forming words and phrases as they changed position along their orbital sky path, glowing between the consonants of the fixed stars. Pythagorean initiates assigned a distinct sound to each sacred vowel…corresponding to the seven realms of Heaven. It was said that blending these seven sacred vowels produced a harmony so pure its tone arose and filled the air in glorious celebration of the Creator.

An early Aramaic alphabet contained 22 letters but no vowels. Elders and teachers orally taught how and when to use each correct pronunciation; indicating which vowel sound within a set of consonants formed the appropriate word. Of these 22 letters, three represented the elements fire, water, air; seven represented the classical planets; and 12 represented the signs of the zodiac. The seven letters assigned to the classical planets were called the "doubles". Each had two sounds with contrasting meanings, interpreted in a context of good or bad, easy or challenging, positive or negative. In modern Western astrology the planets also represent dual influences which require careful interpretation within context, much like the oral language spoken by the ancients.

TALES OF THE CONSTELLATIONS

Early humankind believed the gods were communicating through the use of a detailed, well-organized system of skywriting; a code which need only be accurately deciphered to provide daily guidance...or perhaps the key to life itself. Priests, royalty, and the upper class were often the most highly educated, and likely to be taught reading and writing, but the messages in the heavens were openly displayed for everyone. To a culture steeped in oral communication, one just beginning to open up to the understanding and use of written language, envisioning messages formed in the sky offered a new frontier of hopeful support from the gods.

Astronomer Claudius Ptolemy, who lived under Roman rule, compiled *Almagest*, a second century body of work including the names he had assigned to 48 constellations. (Today 88 constellations are officially recognized by the

International Astronomical Union, including most of the early names contributed by Ptolemy.) Patterns formed by star groupings created an ancient sky map, weaving a tapestry that came alive through glorious mythical tales. These starry outlines served as guideposts, boundaries, and reference markers; useful for tracking celestial motion..."a picture is worth a thousand words."

Constellations divided the sky into manageable viewing sectors. And through their colorful tales, the language of the sky thrived and spread as a universally meaningful reference passed down through time. Many constellations are associated with mythical stories from the Greeks and Romans; mnemonic lessons etched into the sky.

Constellations were placed in meaningful patterns; their tales often interwoven. One such example is the myth of Queen Cassiopeia, who boasted her daughter Andromeda was more beautiful than the Nereides, the sea nymphs who protected sailors and fishermen. This angered the Nereides who called on the sea god Poseidon for vengeance. Poseidon threatened to ravage the land of King Cepheus and Queen Cassiopeia. To save his kingdom, Cepheus agreed to sacrifice his daughter, and chained her to the rocks as an offering to the sea monster Cetus. Andromeda awaited her wretched fate as Cetus drew near.

Luckily (as happens in great stories) there was a hero nearby who saw this damsel in distress. Perseus, riding the winged horse Pegasus, was returning to Greece from his latest quest—to bring back the head of the Medusa Gorgon. Perseus did what heroes have always done…he flew to her rescue and slew the beastly Cetus. Perseus and Andromeda were married, and upon their deaths they were placed in the sky as glowing constellations on either side of Cassiopeia. Three other characters from this story also take their place near Cassiopeia. King Cepheus sits next to his Queen, while the sea monster Cetus looms close by, and Pegasus, the winged horse ridden by heroic Perseus, appears not far away. One story, six characters: Perseus, Andromeda, Cassiopeia, Cepheus, Cetus, and Pegasus, forever entwined, etched in the stars as one memorable section of the sky, their story repeated for thousands of years.

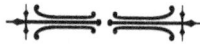

⊢═══ ═══⊣

Constellations are like books on a library shelf. They are filled with wonderful stories, but must be acknowledged and "read" to grasp their deeper meaning. When constellations are viewed with an imaginative mind they morph from crude form into spectacular story. Stars are guided into outlines, as in a game of "connect the dots"; reminiscent of times when we, as children, lay on our backs in the warm summer grass and looked up to find meaningful shapes in the clouds. Stories were told to describe the constellations, for when a story is told the mind's eye remembers.

Lyra honors the memory of Orpheus and his musical lyre; *Corona Borealis*, the "Northern Crown" represents the magnificent jeweled crown King Minos's daughter Ariadne wore at her wedding to the wine god Dionysus. The demigod Hercules, immortalized for his many heroic deeds, lies between *Lyra* and *Corona Borealis*. The 12 constellations familiar to us as the astrological signs of the zodiac appear in the sky along the great circle called the ecliptic path, marking the sun's annual journey.

Seven stars in the shape of an hourglass define the constellation *Orion*, the mighty hunter who stands in the night sky with the bright star *Sirius*, the *Dog Star* (his faithful companion) at his feet. The stars Betelgeuse and Bellatrix shine as Orion's shoulders, and Rigel and Saiph mark his feet, completing the outer lines of his body. Midway in the formation is the familiar *Belt of Orion*...three bright stars in a row: Mintaka, Alnilam, and Alnitak.

The *Belt of Orion* is an asterism; a group of stars which form a recognizable pattern other than a constellation. Asterisms appear within a single constellation, or cross into neighboring constellations. The *Big Dipper* is an asterism formed by the upper hindquarter and tail of the constellation *Ursa Major*, the *Great Bear*. The *Little Dipper* is found in *Ursa Minor*, the *Little Bear*, with the tail as its handle, and the bear's flank as its bowl. The *Pleiades*, or *Seven Sisters*, are part of the constellation Taurus. The *Summer Triangle* is an asterism composed of three bright stars (*Vega, Deneb, Altair*), each star from a separate constellation (*Lyra, Cygnus,* and *Aquila*).

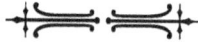

During the early Roman Empire the northern hemisphere was the natural vantage point for viewing. The sky and constellations in that sector reflect their cultural myths of old. Centuries later star groupings, especially those in the southern hemisphere, were identified and named to reflect more current themes: scientific, industrial, and artistic. The constellations: *Microscopium*, the microscope; *Telescopium*, the telescope; *Antlia*, the air pump; *Horologium*, the clock; *Pictor*, the painter; *Sculptor*; and *Caelum*, the sculptor's chisel, are several which fit these themes—named in the 18th century by French astronomer Abbé Nicolas Louis de Lacaille. (According to the International Astronomical Union (IAU) 20th century astronomers opted to use an official set of constellation boundaries by sky coordinates rather than star pattern or shape…yet the old stories live on.)

PRACTICAL GUIDANCE

The language of the sky is more than an ancient oracle offering sage advice to a select few; more than a riddle or code for scientists to decipher. The universe "speaks" to everyone, offering guidance on a daily basis to those who choose to see...and listen. Early humans were nomadic, migrating in search of food and shelter for survival. As humankind evolved toward a localized culture, survival tactics shifted from searching, to establishing nearby sustainable sources of food and shelter. Reliable cultivation of crops and livestock became paramount to the foundation and preservation of a society; and the gods played a key role.

The Romans honored Saturn, god of agriculture; patron of an industry relying on timing, cycles, and patterns to assure fertile cultivation and a plentiful bounty. Renderings of Saturn often depict him carrying a sickle; his symbolic instrument of an abundant harvest. The ancient Roman festival Saturnalia lasted for several days during mid-December, near the winter solstice. It was a celebration of a bountiful harvest, and a time given to merrymaking and relaxed social order. Courts and schools were closed, lavish banquets held, and gifts were exchanged. Slaves were treated as family and honored guests by their masters, enjoying measures of freedom and behavior not usually allowed. Saturnalia was a mix of sacred time to honor their god of agriculture, and commercial gift-giving, feasting, and merriment; inklings of a pattern trickled down to our modern day winter holiday and festive season.

Holding festivities and offering sacrifice to appease the gods was not enough to ensure necessary water supply, sunshine, or warm temperatures needed to produce plentiful crops and healthy livestock. Humankind's inability to control nature posed costly and deadly risks. But learning to forecast weather patterns, time agricultural cycles, and predict the likelihood of harmful infestation or disease lessened the odds stacked against them. Immersed in a world offering countless clues early humankind instinctively sought guidance and inspiration from their surroundings.

LUNAR CYCLES

Celestial cycles were monitored, and aligned with events for forecasting and timing. Shorter cycles naturally provided quicker understanding. Among the seven viewable classical planets, the span of one lunar month (approximately 29 days to complete its phases from new moon to full moon and back to the next new moon) proved especially useful. The moon's timing was honored in the ancient tale of the Greek Titan moon goddess, Selene. Homer's *Hymn to Selene* paints the scene: "From her immortal head a radiance is shown from heaven and embraces earth...her rays beam clear, whensoever bright Selene...drives on her long-maned horses at full speed, at eventime in the mid-month; then her great orbit is full and then her beams shine brightest as she increases. So she is a sure token and sign to mortal men."

The phases of the moon, so poetically captured by Homer, were beneficial indicators of timing. Tracking events during each lunar phase, drawing correlations, and recording conclusions produced a valuable reference that evolved with time. "As above, so below" was anticipated. Using lunar cycles wasn't unique to the Roman Empire; reliance on the moon was practiced around the world.

Native American tribes named each full moon to coincide with seasonal observances; tracking and monitoring the passage of time through the year, from one lunar cycle to the next. European settlers assigned full moon names of their own to reflect the orderly completion of tasks. Algonquins called the March full moon "Worm Moon", signaling the return of the robin; or "Crow Moon" when the sound of cawing crows indicated the end of winter was near. That same March full moon was called "Sap Moon" or "Sugar Moon" by northeastern settlers; a reminder it was time to tap the maple trees for their sweet, vital fluid. The full moon nearest the autumnal equinox was called "Harvest Moon". Its glow provided light well into the evening hours, allowing more time to work in the fields and gather crops for storage to last through the long winter ahead.

RULES OF THUMB

Time syncs itself to no one. Alignment with lunar cycles required periodic adjustment to keep the full moon names associated with their designated tasks. Generally three full moons appear in each season: spring, summer, autumn, winter; but occasionally the 29-day lunar cycle produces a fourth full moon within a season. To overlook this phenomenon and continue using the next full moon name in sequence throws off the tasking schedule. A "rule of thumb" was instituted as a reminder to alleviate discrepancies caused by an "extra" seasonal full moon. The *Maine Farmer's Almanac* stated that the number of full moons should be counted from the beginning of each season. When any season has a fourth full moon, the third of those four full moons is "skipped" and called "Blue Moon" as a marker, which kept the remaining names in alignment with their associated tasks.

Some say "Blue Moon" was chosen as a reference to those rare times in history when the moon did indeed appear blue in color due to some natural phenomenon: the 1883 eruption of Krakatoa, whose ash gave a blue colored haze to the moon; the excessive dust from the 1927 late arrival of the monsoon season in India which cast a blue hue against the moon; and when the smoke from the 1951 forest fires in western Canada filled the sky, giving the moon a blue color.

Like myth, rules of thumb can be misinterpreted or misunderstood. A 1946 magazine article written by an amateur astronomer linked the term "Blue Moon" to the appearance of a second full moon within any calendar month (not season). His story was published in the popular *Sky & Telescope* magazine and the rest is history...or folklore.

His misinterpretation took hold and quickly spread as a conventional rule of thumb. (Hermes, the messenger god who oversees communication, the trickster who loves a practical joke, surely had his hand in this.) The modern western world was well adept at scheduling and tracking tasks and so, for most, this inadvertent adaptation to an age old practice went unnoticed; little more than a ripple moving through time.

LUNAR GARDENING

Lunar gardening is another moon-associated tradition carried over from ancient times. This agricultural practice aligns phases of the moon with tasks: soil preparation, planting, cultivation, and harvesting cycles. Years of practical application and research have demonstrated the effect various moon phases have on crops; suggesting such details as best lunar phases to plant above ground crops versus root crops, and beneficial care for plants during each phase of the lunar cycle (watering, pruning, etc.).

Many of our nation's forefathers were farmers who kept a watchful eye on the sky. In the 18th century it was Ben Franklin who, writing under the pseudonym Richard Saunders, published his *Poor Richard's Almanack*, a helpful aid with a variety of useful information. Beyond gardening tips, his *Almanack* covered astronomical and astrological data, weather forecasting, even clever sayings, anecdotes, and bits of wisdom. Franklin's *Almanack* ceased publication in the 18th century, but other versions of a farmer's almanac continue to this day, offering many of the same topics as the original.

Weather and nature play key roles in our lives. We have long accepted that oceanic tides are affected by the gravitational pull of the moon and, to a lesser extent, the sun. The highest and lowest tides occur at the full moon and at the new moon, when the combined gravitational pull of the moon and sun is heightened due to their relative position to each other. But more than tides are affected. Groundwater tables beneath the earth's surface are also affected by gravitational pull; lower at the last phase before a new moon, pulling less moisture to the surface and producing drier soil conditions, and higher near the full moon when more moisture is drawn to the surface.

CELESTIAL PHENOMENA

New words were added as humankind embraced the role of celestial bodies in daily life. "Disaster" (ill-starred) described terrible events believed to be caused from above; "influenza" (influence of the stars) blamed the cause of an illness on occult forces.

Eclipses, when viewed as harbingers of misfortune, were feared by many ancient cultures; a solar eclipse appeared to some as if a dragon were swallowing the sun. Fearing that its life-giving light would be extinguished, flaming arrows were shot skyward to scare off the monstrous beast and relight the sun. Solar eclipses occur only at a new moon, when the moon passes between sun and Earth. Lunar eclipses occur only at a full moon, when Earth is between the moon and sun. Eclipses of either kind were interpreted with great care; their significance as herald of good fortune, or as portent of bad omen—foreshadowing times of famine, disease, and war were taken quite seriously.

Comets were both feared and welcomed by the ancients; appearing suddenly and infrequently, becoming larger in size as they approached, traveling across the sky pulling their long tails. Some comets pass through a viewing area of the sky only once; others are periodic. Halley's comet for example, orbits the sun and predictably returns to view. NASA poetically described this phenomenon as "a messenger from the dawn of the universe".

Closer to home, the beautiful sight of a gloriously colored rainbow is a welcome spectacle; an omen stirring tales of luck and leprechauns, a pot of gold rumored found at its end. In Greek myth Iris is the messenger goddess (frequently doing Hera's bidding) who used the rainbow as her pathway between Heaven and Earth. A rainbow appeared as she traveled to Earth and disappeared just as quickly upon her leave. A rainbow seen arcing into the sea was said to be the goddess Iris replenishing the rain clouds from earthly waters.

Mythical Iris offers humankind her full spectrum of color; from the glorious sight of her rainbow to lending her name to the colored part of the human eye. The eye's iris controls the size of its pupil by muscle expansion and contraction, allowing in outer light to help us see more clearly. Iris, the messenger goddess, enlightened students of the gods ("pupils") by delivering divine messages. The tears we cry are reminiscent of the salty seas Iris used to replenish the moisture in the clouds. It is with the help of Iris that we see what is before us and receive the god's messages.

ANCIENT OBSERVATORIES

Early civilizations developed sophisticated means by which to read the sky. Observatories were constructed with great care and precision, in purposeful and deliberate detail, and for optimum accuracy. Kokino, the 4,000 year old megalithic observatory discovered in Macedonia in 1991, has been ranked by NASA as the fourth oldest ancient observatory in the world. Described as the "Macedonian Stonehenge", research indicates Kokino contained specially designed openings through which the movement of the sun and the moon could be monitored. Parts of this observatory are so well preserved it is still possible to mark the sun's position during the summer solstice.

Ancient sites throughout the world have been identified as possible observatories; purposefully built in alignment with celestial objects and events. Abu Simbel, a temple built in Egypt under the rule of King Ramses II, dates back to 13th century BCE and is rumored to be oriented so that twice a year (on the date of the King's birthday in February and again on the date of his coronation in October), the rays of the morning sun shine into the temple and illuminate four statues along its back wall.

Stonehenge, the ancient megalithic monument in Great Britain is speculated to have been used as a site for religious ceremony or as an observatory. Another, the Newgrange Megalithic Passage Tomb in Ireland, dates back to 3200 BCE and has a chamber that is illuminated by the sunrise of the winter solstice. Used as a modern-day tourist attraction, admission to the winter solstice sunrise event is determined in September of each year…by lottery drawing. Fifty names are drawn from thousands entered, and two places per name are awarded for the viewing.

HEAVENLY MUSIC

Pythagoras looked to the heavens and envisioned an acoustic monochord; one string, a single thread connecting spirit (Heaven) and matter (Earth). Believing music and harmony had a mathematical relationship, he studied the science of harmonics: oscillations, intervals, and frequencies. He applied his theory of harmonics to the planets, assigning to each one either a tone or half-tone. Pythagoras was said to have heard the "music of the spheres", harmonious celestial tones resonating from above; sounds more sublime than mortal man could ever create.

Modern humankind left the ancient's earthly vantage point and ventured forth, reaching out into the heavens to capture the sounds of celestial music. During its space exploration mission NASA's Voyager craft sent back recordings of sounds captured from the atmospheres of the outer planets. Each planet had a distinctive musical pattern which appeared to have a calming affect on its listener. Called "Ion Acoustic Waves" by NASA, these vibrational frequencies within the range of normal human hearing have been referred to as the "real music of the spheres". They are being studied for their similarity to "primordial sounds"—those soothing ever-present sounds of life within our own body: heartbeat, breath, and blood flow.

Natural phenomena in Earth's own atmosphere produce radio emissions referred to by scientists as "tweeks", "whistlers", and "sferics" (short for atmospherics). Many of Earth's natural radio emissions can be converted to audible sound waves through a simple very low frequency (VLF) radio receiver, easily constructed with an antenna and audio amplifier. Immersed in nature we exist within our own daily theater, complete with "surround sound"; from the boom of thunder and crackle of lightning, to the breathtaking beauty of the charged plasma particles of the solar wind which create the northern lights—aurora borealis—named in honor of the Roman goddess of the dawn "Aurora" and the Greek north wind "Boreas".

TO THE HEART OF STORY

Stories personifying and animating the sky have been passed down through the ages. The *Homeric Hymns* tell of Helios (Sun), and Selene (Moon); many folktales describe the "man in the moon"...or the "hare". Our own childhood memories hold storied explanations for the weather—a crash of loud thunder, we are told, is the sound of angels bowling. The value and lesson in any story is ours to discover. Some look beyond obvious morals or mere entertainment to find personal connections linking delightful bits of wondrous fantasy to images sprinkled about our everyday world. In my own childhood, this would be the story of *Frau Holle* (Mother Hulda), from the 19th century *Household Tales* collection by the Brothers Grimm.

The story begins with a familiar cast: a widow, her favored ugly, lazy daughter, and her beautiful, hardworking stepdaughter (the one who slaved over household chores). One day as the stepdaughter sat near a well, busily weaving, she lost her spinning shuttle down the well and jumped in to retrieve it. Down, down she fell, landing in a fantasy world with flowered meadows, a baker's oven filled with loaves of bread begging her to take them out before they burned, and a tree weighted down with fruit asking her to shake it and gather its ripe apples. All these tasks she graciously completed.

As the girl wandered about this wondrous new land she happened on an old woman's cottage. The old woman who lived there, Frau Holle, bade the girl to stay and help with the household chores; taking special care to "...make my bed well, and shake it thoroughly till the feathers fly—for then there is snow on the earth". The girl obeyed and "...always shook her bed so vigorously that the feathers flew about like snowflakes". So pleased was Frau Holle that when the girl prepared to return to her own family she was rewarded for her hard work with a shower of gold.

When the girl arrived home she told her adventurous tale; and the greedy, lazy stepsister set out down the well to claim her own fortune in gold. She passed the baker's oven and refused to remove its bread; she heard the cries from the fruit tree and would not shake loose and gather its apples. She arrived at the old woman's cottage and was invited to stay and help with the chores. She too was instructed to shake out the feather bed and make the snow fly. But the lazy girl did not do her chores, and the snow did not fly as it should. Frau

Holle was quite displeased with the lazy girl and promptly dismissed her; sending her home covered, not in a shower of gold, but in a layer of pitch.

Now the moral of this story may very well be that an honest day's work will be rewarded. But this tale was oft repeated during my childhood for a very different reason—as explanation for the beautiful crystalline snowflakes floating down from the sky. The fairy tale holds this precious seed: when snowflakes fall on a winter's day, smile and know all is well...Frau Holle has the good maid that day!

We too look to the sky for answers; to discover clues which may help us determine how we should dress, and what activities are favored in concert with the conditions. We arise in the morning and look up at the sky for inklings of what the day's weather may hold...sunny, rainy, warm, cold? We recite the familiar rhyming mnemonic: "Red sky at night, sailor's delight; red sky at morning, sailor take warning.". We would much prefer the pleasant experience of a summer's picnic on a warm, sunny day than on a cold, blustery, rainy afternoon. And why bother to don galoshes and an overcoat, or open an umbrella when there is no hint of rain?

WRITTEN ACROSS THE SKY

Following in the footsteps of the ancient gods we claim the sky as our personal stationery. Cloud writing and night skywriting are produced by searchlights or lasers projecting images from the ground against the clouds and evening sky. In daylight, airplanes dispense a mixture of smoke and oil from a plane's exhaust to create deliberate character formations. Guided by the pilot's skillful flight, brief messages are crafted "above" which can be seen on the ground "below" for miles.

We see what the ancients saw…rich stories etched in the form of constellations; a few of our own descriptions added since then. Modern day stargazers acknowledge identifying the constellation Cassiopeia by its resemblance to the English alphabet letter "W".

Look through the lens of your heart and you too may see the gods' storied messages written across the sky. Each movement we make guides our mythic fated thread to form a unique pattern to complete the embroidered outline of our own personal constellation. If we honor our life story there is hope that one day, a long time from now, tales of our heroic adventures will be cast into the heavens; and we shall be forever immortalized among the twinkling stars.

Listen with the expectation to hear and you may be blessed to hear the distant sounds of the music of the spheres known to Pythagoras. Humankind's connection with the sky is told by every cloud with a silver lining, each wish upon a star; whether we shoot the moon, or search for that elusive pot of gold at the end of the rainbow.

CHAPTER SEVEN

MARKING TIME

The only reason for time is so that everything
doesn't happen at once
~ Albert Einstein

" A time to be born and a time to die"…familiar words from the King James Bible, Ecclesiastes 3:2, which serve as markers to measure the span of life; the length of which has been determined by the Moirai, the Fates. The body passes on. The spirit is kept alive through legacies: children, accomplishments, and contributions. There are moments in life when our passion is ignited with such spark that we surpass ordinary achievement and capture a glimpse of immortality; so in sync with the rhythm of the universe that time, ever so briefly, stands still.

Khronos (Chronus, Aeon), is the ancient Greek personi-fication of eternal time…time that has always been; existing before Chaos, the vast darkness from which came the creation of Gaia the Earth, and Ouranos the Sky. Time is that space in which all of nature and humankind exist; elusive, fleeting, and yet we cannot help but chase it, and race against that which waits for no man. Searching for creative ways to track, manipulate, outwit, and capture time (our elusive friend and occasional foe), has become our passion…and obsession.

COUNTING TIME

Chronology (akin to the ancient god Chronus, eternal time) is the process of placing events in an orderly sequence through time; a way for us to measure the duration of our existence. For thousands of years humankind has been captivated with keeping time, assessing its passing, and foreshadowing its end. Archaeologists dated fossilized notched animal bones and sticks, believed to have been used to track lunar phases, back to the Ice Age.

Recording cycles of celestial bodies formed the basis for ancient calendars; an accounting of the days. Many early calendars were either lunar (following moon phases), or lunisolar (based on moon phases but periodically corrected by the addition of extra days or a thirteenth month to bring it back into sync with the seasons).

"Beware the Ides of March", forebodingly warned the soothsayer to Julius Caesar in Shakespeare's play. The omen came not because this date was considered generally ominous, but because the soothsayer foresaw this particular time in March could prove personally perilous to Caesar.

The early Roman calendar referenced days of the month by three distinct times; each of which was used as a marker for counting the rest of the month. These were: Kalends (1st day of the month); Nones (the 7th day in March, May, July, and October; the 5th in other months); and Ides (the 15th day in March, May, July, and October; the 13th in other months). The remaining days of the month were identified by where they fell in relation to one of these major three dates. (Two days before Nones, for example.)

A variety of calendars evolved across cultures. The Egyptians devised a calendar based on the rising of Sirius, the "Dog Star" in the constellation Canis Major. Sirius was visible above the horizon just before sunrise each year around the time the Nile River would flood. The Nile's receded waters left behind a rich silt, signaling a time of fertile fields. And the Mayans were guided by a series of calendars based on lunar, solar, and Venus cycles.

Solar calendars were a means of maintaining synchronicity with the tropical year (seasons) by periodically adding in days to create leap years; they gained popularity during the time of Julius Caesar. The modern-day Gregorian calendar, named for Pope Gregory XIII who decreed its use in the 16th century, modified the Julian calendar to adjust for greater accuracy.

The quest for precise timing led to a multitude of ways to mark time. Elaborate sundials were built as stone pillar obelisks erected to cast a shadow which moved with the sun as it traveled across the daily sky. Etchings and markings carved around the base of the tower were touched by sunlight and shade, indicating intervals of time. Sundials were useful on clear days but were ineffective during nighttime hours or on overcast days, when lack of sunlight cast no shadow.

A timing device which required no sunlight was the water clock ("clepsydra" or water thief). As it slowly dripped water (or mercury) from a small hole in its vessel, time was determined by reading the liquid's level aligned with markings inside the structure of its bowl. In the third century BCE the Greeks made an early version of an alarm clock by using clepsydras that triggered a whistle upon reaching a calibrated level. Adding gears and feedback mechanisms to the clepsydra improved accuracy by regulating a more constant rate of liquid flow; if the vessel was left undisturbed.

Aboard ships the practicality of keeping a steady clepsydra was nearly impossible; the liquid in the timing bowl sloshed with the rise and fall of the ship as it cut through rough sea waves. But nature offered other resources to assist in the telling of time. In daylight, the position and movement of the sun was helpful. And for marking nighttime hours a star clock, called a merkhet, was devised. The merkhet was a rather simple instrument made by fastening a hanging plumb line to a rod and forming a north-south alignment with Polaris, the Pole Star. Time was determined by measuring intervals when designated stars crossed the merkhet's alignment with the Pole Star.

Natural elements (sunlight, wind, water) starred in the architectural design called the "Tower of the Winds"; constructed in the first or second century BCE under the supervision of the Greek astronomer Andronikos. The ruins of this glorious octagonal structure, a modern-day tourist attraction, stands in Athens and rises nearly 50 feet in height, with sundials, and internal water clock (clepsydra). When originally built, a wind-directed weather vane sat atop the tower.

The Anemoi are the seasonal winds from Greek myth. They are honored in sculpture on their directional side of the tower; with minor winds aptly placed alongside. Personified as male deities these eight winds are: Boreas, the cold and powerful winter north wind; Euros (Eurus), the stormy autumnal east wind; Notos (Notus), the summer storm indicator of risky sailing south wind; Zephyros (Zephyrus), the pleasant spring breezes west wind; Kaikias, the dark northeast wind bringer of snow and hail; Apeliotes (Apeliotus), the southeast wind of refreshing rains; Lips (Livos), the warm southwest wind who ushers smooth sailing; and Skiron (Skeiron), the northwest wind whose presence signals the onset of winter.

PERSONIFICATION OF TIMEPIECES

As humankind evolved so too did the desire for more sophisticated timepieces. Mere functionality was no longer enough; clocks became beautifully crafted works of art with enhanced features: ringing bells, doors which opened and closed, and figurines which moved about. The 16th century hailed the introduction of spring-powered and smaller, more portable clocks and watches. The 17th century saw the addition of minute hands, and the creation of pendulum clocks. Fascination with time extended throughout the world. During the 18th century, the southern hemisphere's constellation Horologium (the clock or timepiece) was charted and named.

Associating parts of a clock with human features awakened a deep-rooted familiarity with our old friend Time. We stare at this harbinger's "face" and "hands" and listen to its soft rhythmic ticking in sync with our own heartbeat; we call them by name. "Grandfather" came from a 19th century Henry Work folk song about a tall pendulum floor clock: "My grandfather's clock was too large for the shelf, so it stood ninety years on the floor.".

"Cuckoo", was named for the distinct call of the native cuckoo bird of Europe whose sound it replicates when a small figurine pops out as the clock strikes the hour or half hour. London's Clock Tower is now called "Elizabeth Tower" to honor Her Majesty the Queen. "Big Ben" is the great bell within that clock whose booming chime resounds far and wide. The name Big Ben was said to have been chosen to honor either the politician Sir Benjamin Hall, or the champion heavyweight boxer Ben Caunt.

Aesthetically, an hourglass shape is associated with the pleasantly curved form of the female figure. An hourglass (sand clock) indicates the passage of time by the changing level of its flowing granules which cascade from its upper chamber and accumulate in a rising pile in its lower. Commonly used in the middle ages aboard ships and in industry, the hour glass in today's world often finds itself relegated to menial tasks as a common kitchen timer, or as a novelty desk ornament for amusement; we sit mesmerized by its flowing grains of sand.

Time is eternal, external, and internal. The "biological clock" describes a personal timing mechanism which influences our circadian rhythms—cyclic self-sustained mental, physical, and behavioral changes stimulated by light and darkness. Circadian rhythms affect sleep cycles, hormone release, metabolic rate, and body temperature. Chronobiology (also akin to Chronus, eternal time) is a science which studies rhythmic timing effects on living organisms.

PROPHECY AND FATE

Time marks the approach of the inevitable; the ticking of a clock counting down the remaining number of our heartbeats. The desire to control aging has us searching for ways to "turn back the hands of time". Manipulating the course of events is something best left to the gods, but even they must submit to the power of the Fates.

Kronos (Cronus), a Titan offspring of Ouranos (Father Sky) and Gaia (Mother Earth), sired the twelve Olympian gods and ruled the heavens. He gained power by deposing his own father, Ouranos; castrating him with the sickle given to him by his mother. In lore, this sickle of Kronos fell from the heavens and landed in Greece at a place called Cape Drepanon; named for its shoreline's crescent shape, taken from the word "drepane" (sickle). The image of Kronos with his sickle stirs a likeness to "Father Time".

The Titan Kronos attempted to thwart the prophecy of his own imminent downfall at the hands of one of his children, by swallowing each child in turn upon their birth. The youngest child, Zeus, was protected by his mother Rhea, who was determined to save this baby from the same terrible fate which had befallen his older siblings. Instead of handing this baby over to Kronos, Rhea gave him a rock wrapped in swaddling. Kronos mistook this rock for his newborn son and swallowed it down, satisfied no child was left to fulfill the dismal prophecy of his doom. Unbeknownst to Kronos, baby Zeus was secretly whisked away to be reared far from the reaches of his Titan father.

Once grown, Zeus returned to the place of his birth and assembled an uprising against his tyrannical father. The Titan Kronos was enticed to drink down a potion which caused him to disgorge those children he had previously swallowed. Freed from within their imprisonment these siblings joined forces, and a fierce battle ensued between the Titans led by Kronos, and the Olympians led by Zeus. It was the younger generation, the Olympians who, aided by the creatures Cyclopes and the 100-armed Giants, prevailed after a lengthy and brutal struggle. Those conquered Titans who fought against the Olympians were banished to Tartarus, the place of torture beneath the Underworld...all save one...the Titan Atlas, who was sentenced to hold up the Heavens, carrying the weight of the world on his shoulders for all eternity.

Take heed all you modern-day "titans of industry", lest you too attempt to stand in time's way and thwart the changing of the guard. A harsh lesson befalls an old regime that suppresses the birthing cries of a new generation; change and progress cannot be stopped. Swallow your pride, not the seeds of the future. Embrace the process of transformation or you too shall endure an epic battle...one you cannot win. For as it was prophesied in ancient times against the Titan Kronos, and his father before him, so too will you be overthrown and cast aside, no longer respected or needed, banished to a place of shame by a new regime. You will be ousted by the innovative thinking and timely progress of youthful creativity; who follow an eternal cycle that must be.

ZONING IN

Caught up in a global desire to control outcomes drives us to manipulate the perception of time to better suit our limited thinking; restructuring our lives, even adjusting circadian rhythms. Time is inevitable, but its human perception is adaptable, to a point. Stretched too far it may snap back with a vengeful force. Time allows humankind their games, pretends to play along, temporarily bending and reshaping its rules to fit the needs of the whole; but Time never truly relinquishes control.

Nineteenth century America brought expansion of train travel and made possible the transport of passengers and goods across vast geographic stretches in a relatively short time. But complications ensued when arrival time was measured by the same clock schedules used for departure time.

Suppose a train trip from Boston to Chicago takes 24 hours. A passenger boards an early Saturday morning train in Boston just as the first rays of sunshine peek above the horizon. He glances at his pocket watch. It is 6:00am when the train departs and he thinks, "Ah, I'll arrive in Chicago at 6:00am Sunday morning, just as the sun is beginning to rise". With that thought he settles in for the long ride. The train arrives in Chicago, right on schedule, 24 hours later, and the passenger looks out to see, not the sunrise but, total darkness. He glances at his watch and reads "6:00am", but where is the sunrise?

He steps off the train and onto the platform in an unfamiliar setting, he and his timepiece out of sync with the present location. Without adjustment, daybreak no longer appears when his watch indicates it should, noon is no longer when the sun is at its highest point in the sky, and sunset seems to be delayed. The passenger stepped off the train into a place of "alternate" time. The advent of progress, traveling long east-west distances (longitudinally), meant bringing more than a change of clothing to suit the new destination. The perception of time needed adjustment.

We are a race of innovative thinkers and it was not long before someone proposed a more practical timing system... worldwide time zones based on Earth's rotation. One such forward thinker was Sir Sanford Fleming, a Scottish-born Canadian engineer who, in the late 19th century, recommended 24 worldwide time zones; each spaced 15 degrees of longitude apart. His reasoning was that with each hour Earth rotated the equivalent of 15 degrees longitude, so by the end of a 24-hour day Earth had completed its entire 360 degree rotational cycle.

Crossing time zones, whether by land, water, or air is "time travel"; for although a constant amount of time passes for the traveler, one could virtually end up in "yesterday" or "tomorrow". Traveling round and round this earthly globe, one can theoretically experience a continual loop of perceptual yesterdays, todays, and tomorrows. Time itself has not changed; only our perception of it.

DAYLIGHT SAVING TIME

A century before the puzzle of time zones was pieced together, an American icon, Benjamin Franklin, toyed with the idea of daylight saving time; a way to cleverly shift the appearance of daylight by manually adjusting clock time. During a 1784 trip to Paris, Franklin drew from personal observation to conceive an economical use of daylight hours. Franklin, well known for his whimsical sense of humor, composed a lengthy letter to the editor of the *JOURNAL DE PARIS*. In his "essay on daylight saving" he offered a witty, tongue-in-cheek accounting of the cost of living by artificial light versus the savings benefit gained by maximizing natural light. Franklin, the man oft associated with the saying: "Early to bed and early to rise, makes a man healthy, wealthy, and wise.", claimed to be astonished that the sun gave off light at the moment of its early rising.

Burning candles was, at the time of his "revelation", the primary source of artificial light for the people of Paris. The ever frugal Franklin calculated the cost of a six month city-wide supply of candle wax and concluded Paris could save "an immense sum" by using sunlight rather than candles. Franklin asked little in return for this marvelous discovery he had gifted to humankind; only that he be given the "honour" of its discovery. "If the ancients knew it, it might have been long since forgotten; for it certainly was unknown to the moderns…", he claimed.

A practical idea wrapped within a clever story, neatly tied up in the words of Benjamin Franklin, author of *Poor Richard's Almanack*. Through humor he broached a sensible solution; one which took many more years before its place in history was accepted. Over the years, daylight saving time guidelines have been enacted and repealed more than once. Proposed start and end dates varied; with some states or geographical portions thereof declining to participate in this makeshift clock time.

Under the 1918 *Act to preserve daylight and provide standard time for the United States*, the practice proved so unpopular it was repealed the following year. During World War II most of the United States adopted year-round daylight saving hours; referring to this period as "War Time". Localities were left to decide whether or not to participate in a daylight saving plan, and when to shift back to standard time, causing much confusion, especially in transportation and communication industries. It wasn't until the federal government enacted The *Uniform Time Act of 1966* that greater standardization across the country was reached.

Having now gained a solid foothold, deeply entrenched in cultural practice, surely poetic justice prevails upon us to call this, not by such a common name—"daylight saving time"—but by something more fittingly descriptive to acknowledge its "discoverer". "Poor Richard's Time" or "Franklin Time" would bestow a memorable legacy upon Benjamin Franklin, granting him the only request he made in return for gifting humankind with this most remarkable contribution…"to have the honour of it".

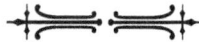

+═──═+

The simple act of moving the hands of a clock…forward or backward…changes the face of time, giving way to a powerful shift; humankind wielding godlike powers. In that very moment when clock time advances one hour in springtime, whether done by few or millions, a shared single hour is snatched and stored in a virtual time vault; imprisoned "somewhere". Was it snatched up by the Harpies and handed over to the ancient deity Chronus (Aeon) for safekeeping? Where does it go? Without a doubt it is held in a most secure place, for our treasured hour always magically reappears when we come back for it in the fall…demanding its return, freeing it from captivity and basking in its leisurely reward of "more time".

Daylight saving time is a shift into alternate time. It's arrival is heralded by great fanfare. Like it or not, we brace ourselves for the ripple it creates in our lives. Symbolic of the labyrinth, we enter into this new dimension and follow along its path until time turns a corner and we are led back to "standard time"; only to repeat this journey the next year, and the next.

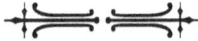

Such a curious thing…time. Again we find ourselves peering into Alice's story as the (Mad) Hatter took his watch out of his pocket, shook it and asked, "What day of the month is it?". Alice replied, "The fourth.". Hatter exclaimed, "Two days wrong!" Alice looked at Hatter's watch and said, "What a funny watch! It tells the day of the month, and doesn't tell what o'clock it is!" Hatter's asked, "Why should it? Does YOUR watch tell you what year it is?"

Lewis Carroll's story was published in 1865, a period when wrist watches were becoming fashionable and readily available for more than just the elite wealthy class. In due course, a calendar was built into the mechanical function of a watch, and time of day merged with calendar days of the year.

When Alice fell into her storied adventures, cultural beliefs once again blended, (or did they collide?) with fantasy.

Time moves us between awake time and dream time; playing its game of cat and mouse. Like the White Rabbit in the Lewis Carroll's, *Alice's Adventures in Wonderland*, we proclaim, "Oh dear! Oh dear! I shall be late!". And so we set a trap to capture a precise moment...one which screams loudly when struck, "alarming" us awake. We perform a ritual of setting these traps to ensure we are "on time" for a variety of reasons: appointments, jobs, school, social engagements; must "get there on time" (wherever "there" is).

SPORTS TIME

The world of sports time is a contradictory, confusing wonderland of its own making; a dimension in space operating unlike any other time we have know, morphing to fit a particular need while following its own set of rules. Gameplay time is a method of guiding action and instilling a sense of urgency by measuring performance based on a numeric formula. "Let the games begin"...sets this beast in motion. The score periodically cries out the standing in this race against the clock.

Time prefers to maintain an air of mystique and changes its appearance, varying with each unique sport. Football, basketball, hockey, soccer: four 15-minute quarters, four

12-minute periods, three 20-minute periods, two 45-minute halfs. Not wanting to seem trite or predictable, Time changes things up for baseball and golf: 9 innings, 19 holes. And tennis is altogether a different matter…best two of three sets, or three of five…with interim scores of "love", "deuce", "advantage"…all depends on Time's mood, I suppose.

Official clock time for a sports event runs out, the game ends, and a winner is declared…or not! If the score is tied at the end of regulation time we enter into that uber-urgent dimension of "overtime"…which may or may not use up all of its officially allotted time. Time is quite serious in this realm, occasionally taking on a form called "sudden death"; a term so final in name one thinks Thanatos, Greek god of death, will appear to whisk away the loser.

Baseball has no allotted clock time. The game extends for as many innings as needed to officially break the tie score. But then there's tennis…ah tennis; some events have no tie break in the final set. The players continue on; minutes become hours, even days, until one player succumbs, and Time mercifully calls an end to the match and declares a winner. Such a lengthy battle may be forever etched in time; a plaque…or statue displayed in commemoration. (Remember the epic Wimbledon 2010 battle between Isner and Mahut?)

Gameplay time twists and stretches the limits of logic: stopping a clock, adding minutes back on to the clock here and there at the discretion of an officiating authority, even granting travel back in time to replay points or review replays, searching for clues missed in "real time".

Down the rabbit hole we go, landing in this wonderland of game time, tempted by refreshments that beckon: "drink me" and "eat this" as we wile away our leisure time. The world of sports time is a place where the clock may show 10 minutes remaining, but we've learned from experience that 10 minutes in this wonderland may be much, much longer when measured against "real time".

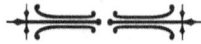

We pass the time, rhythmically keep time, spend time, waste time, save time, "do" time as repentance for societal wrongdoings, and punish our children with time outs. Time flies, we lose track of time, march to double time, and two-time in our relationships. We mark the length of our experience on this earth by measuring how much time has passed between, and since memorable events; counting birthdays, anniversaries, years of service, until such time as the image of Kronos with his sickle conjures Father Time, the Grim Reaper. A stirring within touches the remembrance of Atropos, the Inevitable Fate who cuts our life's thread; and we pass on, perhaps to that secure place which holds our precious daylight saving hour—another time. "To every thing there is a season, and a time to every purpose under the heaven."

CHAPTER EIGHT

A SENSE OF GUIDANCE

Do not follow where the path may lead.
Go instead where there is no path and leave a trail
~ Ralph Waldo Emerson

Theseus found his way out of the labyrinth by following his clew of thread. Dorothy followed the Yellow Brick Road and discovered "there's no place like home". In story and in life we are on a continual journey to find our way—from here to there—discovering new and innovative sources of guidance, searching for what lies beyond. Eagerly anticipating the adventure we expect to find what we seek "just around the next corner". A powerful mix of curiosity and necessity fuels our desire to revisit the tried and true, improvise, and explore new frontiers.

In *Hansel and Gretel*, the Brothers Grimm tale, Hansel overheard his wicked stepmother's plot to abandon the children in the woods, and prepared by gathering pebbles the night before. As they were led away he dropped the pebbles to mark a trail so he and Gretel could retrace their steps out of the forest; a clever strategy which worked quite well. But, Hansel and Gretel were not so fortunate the second time they were abandoned in the woods. The wicked stepmother locked the door and Hansel was unable to sneak outside and gather pebbles as he had done before. His recent success still fresh in his mind, Hansel quickly improvised to mark a new trail with what he had on hand...bread. He tore off and dropped bits of bread as he walked along; discovering, not the way home, but that adaptation doesn't always produce the same results as the original.

Now those familiar with this tale know full well how Hansel fared with his bread crumb trail...the trail disappeared as quickly as it had been created. The morsels were picked up by the birds, and we traveled along with Hansel and Gretel on a fantastic roundabout journey of discovery which, admittedly, ended quite well. Yes, necessity is indeed the mother of invention, for if Hansel had been able to successfully repeat his original trail marking method then we might not have stumbled upon the great discovery of the delicious gingerbread house, nor found the treasure chests filled with pearls and jewels, before returning home to "happily ever after".

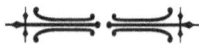

The breadcrumb trail has made its way into our lives, perhaps inspired by Hansel's own innovative guidance system.

A computer software navigational aid called "breadcrumbs" is a tool designed to link back to previous pages...allowing the user ease in retracing steps. The story of Hansel & Gretel is known throughout the world; equally so is the knowledge that Hansel's breadcrumbs idea was "for the birds" and yielded unexpected results. Given the obvious difficulties faced by our much beloved Hansel & Gretel, why name a navigational software aid "breadcrumbs"? Was the intent to abandon us in a forest of technology, to strand us in an unfamiliar place, left to encounter a great adventure before finding our way home? And will we fare as well from our journey into the unknown as did the children in the Brothers Grimm fairy tale?

CELESTIAL NAVIGATION

We are driven, to find "places" and "things", whether by necessity or curiosity. To ensure successfully repeating a favorable experience (reaching from point A to point B) usually requires a plan...plotting a course, establishing a route...remembering what has gone before. Ancient seekers often relied on nature's guidance. Set patterns and reliable constants were noted and observed, then studied with contemplative reflection. Whether sailing the seas or traveling across land, survival depended on one's sense of guidance.

During daylight hours the sun's position often guided, and at night the moon and stars took center stage. Celestial navigation (navigating by the sky) is an ancient skill, a craft which evolved into a complex science of discovery; bolstered by maps and the invention of instruments such as sextants, compasses, and Global Positioning Systems (GPS).

In the Northern hemisphere the star formations: Big Dipper, Little Dipper, and Cassiopeia are visible year round. The North Star (also called Polaris or the Pole Star), shines as the last star in the handle of the Little Dipper—half way between the Big Dipper and Cassiopeia. This bright star appears to remain constant or fixed while other stars travel around it, and is frequently used as a reliable reference to gain one's bearings. In the Southern Hemisphere (where the North Star is not visible) navigators use star points in the Southern Cross (Crux) constellation for guidance.

The path of the sun rises in the east and sets in the west. The first waxing crescent of a new moon appears in the western sky darkened by the setting sun, and a full moon rises in the east as the sun sets in the west. History recorded sundials aboard Viking ships, and ancient lore tells of the use of sunstones—rock crystals which could locate the sun even when it was hidden from view by clouds or fog. As the crystal was held up to the sky, the sun's polarized beams passed through it, creating a natural reference point to locate the sun. The Norse hero Sigurd is mentioned in story using such a magical stone for guidance.

A NATURAL COURSE

Humankind's reliance on nature for navigational aid crosses time. Sailors, airplane pilots, automobile drivers, and hikers use landmarks and topography to judge their position. But they also use instrumentation, radio beacons, and satellite...perhaps also inspired by nature. Marine animals use the topography of the ocean floor or other physical formations to find their way. Whales bounce sonar signals off underwater objects to identify shape and movement, and to determine location. Sea turtles can pick up the earth's magnetic field. Sharks use electrolocation (weak electrical fields) to sense objects...those to steer clear of...and those to hone in on as prey. A shark traveling in shallow water might even use the sky for navigation.

⊹≈≈⊹

Modern humans may find polarized sunglasses useful for reducing glare, but to creatures like the butterfly (and in the legend of the Viking sunstone), polarization is a critical navigational tool. The Monarch butterfly has a light-detecting sensor within, which picks up the sun's polarized ultraviolet rays; allowing the butterfly to detect the angle of the sun, fly south for migration, and return home.

Honey bees have been studied to determine how they search for a food source, return to the hive, and alert other bees to the exact location of their newly found discovery. One conclusion was that honey bees use the sun as a compass or reference point to provide a fixed angle for orientation and navigation. Once a food source was located, the bee returned to the hive and "danced" locational directions to others in the hive through a choreographed tail wagging routine.

The Indigo Bunting bird migrates at night, using stars for guidance. Artificial light has been shown to disorient and trick birds into flying in the wrong direction. Experiments conducted inside a planetarium demonstrated the birds' ability to "learn" a sky map from which to orient their migratory flight pattern. Wind direction has also been mentioned as a possible navigational source used by some birds.

The service of Homing pigeons (messenger or carrier pigeons), has been enlisted since ancient times. The birds were released to herald the arrival of a distinguished caller, or to carry battle messages informing of surrender or defeat. The Mongol ruler Ghengis Khan was said to have used pigeons as a communication system throughout his empire during the 12th and 13th centuries. The 19th century news of Napoleon's defeat at Waterloo was received in England via carrier pigeon; and homing pigeons were widely used in both modern-era World Wars.

How do birds find their way to a given destination and back...at times even crossing continents? For guidance in familiar home territory pigeons are believed to use landmarks and visually recognizable clues, and a sense of smell to hone in on a location. On longer flights, pigeons, inclined to roost at night, use the position of the sun and their own internal circadian clock. Scientists are studying the possibility of an internal compass located in a pigeon's head which locks onto the earth's magnetic field.

For many centuries, we have relied on simple man-made versions of a compass device; nothing more than a magnetized needle on a pivot. When unobstructed, the compass needle points north by aligning with Earth's natural magnetic field. Under certain conditions Earth's terrain produces its own natural compass, of sorts; physical markings which can be used for guidance. In arid desert-like stretches with little or no vegetation cracks in the gravelly-covered land followed a north-south configuration. The blazing heat from the sun can create enough pressure to split apart rock surfaces in a very telling way. In the desert southwest (United States) a research sampling indicated a majority of cracks on round uniform boulders followed the north-south alignment.

DIVINE GUIDANCE

Nature leads the way by example, and an astute observer takes her cue. Civilizations developed an intricate system of trails and roadways, then compiled this data into a catalog…the atlas…a collection of maps referenced to maneuver through a maze of city streets and across terrain. The Titan Atlas is the one said to have taught humankind the art of astronomy; a skill used in navigation, and in seasonal crop cultivation.

In Greek myth Atlas fathered the seven sisters collectively known as the Pleiades. They were placed into the sky by Zeus, as a star cluster in the constellation Taurus, visible in the Northern Hemisphere for only part of the year. The ancient Greeks were guided by the Pleiades's appearance and disappearance to signal the beginning and end of the calm sailing season, as well as for agricultural timing.

The poet Hesiod, in his *Works and Days*, mentions their important role: "When the Pleiades Atlagenes (born of Atlas) are rising begin your harvest, and your ploughing when they are going to set. Forty nights and days they are hidden and appear again as the year moves round, when first you sharpen your sickle." As for sailing, Hesiod warns: "…if desire for uncomfortable sea-faring seize you; when the Pleiades plunge into the misty sea to escape Oarion's rude strength, then truly gales of all kinds rage."

Seafarers were familiar with the celestial phenomenon known as "St. Elmo's Fire"; a luminous blue flamelike glow around ships' masts, often seen during the waning of a thunderstorm. The appearance of St. Elmo's Fire was viewed as a good omen by ancient mariners; interpreted as a visit by the Dioskouroi—the twins Kastor and Polydeukes (Castor and Pollux), protectors of sailors. Homer speaks of the Dioskouroi (Dioscuri) in Hymn as being: "...deliverers of men on earth and of swift-going ships when stormy gales rage over the ruthless sea.". In answer to the prayers of seafarers, "..these two are seen darting through the air on tawny wings...fair signs are they and deliverance from toil. And when the shipmen see them they are glad and have rest from their pain and labour.".

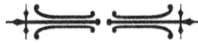

⊢⊇ ⊆⊣

The Titan Atlas inspired stories by Homer, Hesiod, Pindar, Ovid. Atlas fought alongside Kronos against the Olympians and when defeated was sentenced to carry the weight of the world (the pillars of heaven) upon his shoulders. Carrying a heavy burden is a lesson long remembered. The Titan's strength and purpose is found within our bodies in the "atlas vertebra"; the first cervical vertebra of the neck, a vital pillar to hold up our dome, the head. At times we too feel as if the "weight of the world" rests upon us, weighing heavily on our minds; supported by our own atlas.

Faith in divine guidance is as natural to humans as instinct is to animals. Ancient Romans believed every man was born into this world with a guardian spirit who accompanied him throughout his lifetime. The Romans called this divine guide "Genius" and celebrated its presence on their birthday with festivities, wine, and wreaths. ("Juno" was the name given to the Roman guardian spirit for women.) Hesiod called the Greek spirits "Daimon" (Daemon), and identified them as people of the Golden Age who, by the will of Zeus, transcended death as spirits to guide mankind. Later stories told that each person was born with two guiding spirits—one who influenced good and the other evil. At the end of one's lifetime a review of a person's deeds determined which of these spirits held greater power over their life.

SURVIVAL WARNINGS

Whether guided by physical senses or whispered to by our Genius, Juno, or Daimon, the ancients left clues for us to follow. The stories they created transport inklings of history, provide entertaining quips, and offer practical guidance. Survival warnings carried within colorful and lively tales are remembered when lessons pounded into the mind through tedious repetition of dull bare facts fade. As story is recalled, the warning repeats in one's mind like the subtle beating of a heart; becoming louder and faster when danger lurks near. As the threat of imminent danger diminishes the lesson fades into the story, all but forgotten, buried beneath the layers of an entertaining tale.

In Greek myth the handsome youth Narcissus attracted many hopeful suitors, but cold-heartedly dismissed them all. One spurned admirer was the mountain nymph Echo, who loved to talk and always tried to get in the last word. Nymphs were Nature spirits, often portrayed as beautiful young maidens, and Zeus frequently dallied among them. One day while Hera was searching for her husband she crossed paths with Echo. Fearing Hera would punish those found with Zeus, Echo sought to detain the goddess through conversation; giving the other nymphs time to flee. Hera realized she had been deceived by Echo, and cursed the nymph with the love of her own speech. Echo was forever thereafter: denied the power to speak the first word, must respond only with another's words, and (as she so desired) would always have the final word.

Echo saw the youth Narcissus in the forest and fell in love with him. But Hera's wicked curse would not allow her to speak her own sentiments; only to repeat his words. Narcissus tired of Echo's game and cruelly rejected her. She fell into despair and wandered in sadness until the physical form of her body faded away, and all that remained was the distant answering sound of her...echo. She is our companion in the mountains, canyons, and caverns; softly repeating our words back to us. Speak to her and she will answer back, but you will never have the final word, for that honor is reserved for the nymph…by the will of the gods.

Many others suffered callous rejection by Narcissus. One distraught youth committed suicide, and as he died he uttered a prayer that Narcissus would one day feel the pain of unrequited love. The avenging goddess Nemesis heard him and granted his dying wish. Narcissus saw his own reflection in a pool of water and became so enamored with the vision that he sat beside the pool, pining for the love of his own reflection. He smiled, and it smiled back; he reached out his arms and its arms reached out. But when he touched the water the vision rippled and faded; yet always returned when the water calmed. Try as he might he could not connect with this elusive lover for whom he so deeply yearned. Narcissus remained seated on the bank near his reflection, an ache in his heart, until he perished. And in that very spot a flower bloomed…the narcissus.

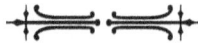

+≈ ≈+

The popular lesson taught from this story cautions on the perils of vanity; a reminder reflected in the word "narcissism", a descriptive term for excessive self-love. But there is another, deeper warning within the story…one of survival. The narcissus is an old world plant native to Europe and the Mediterranean region; its beautiful flower has also been called daffodil. The sap from this flower is highly toxic, not only to people and animals, but to other flowers (as was the storied youth Narcissus to those who fell in love with him). Many of the youth's suitors were identified as nymphs—Nature Spirits—personified plants. In real life, narcissus or daffodil flowers cut for display are specially treated, or kept separate in water for many hours to dissipate the potency of their natural toxins before other plant varieties can be safely introduced into the vase.

The bulbous root of the narcissus and daffodil are highly poisonous and can be easily mistaken in appearance for the edible eating onion or shallot. (The youth Narcissus was fooled by his own deadly reflection!) It is not uncommon to hear reports of accidental poisoning because someone mistakenly used the bulb of the narcissus or daffodil in place of an edible onion in food preparation.

To an ancient culture of gatherers, stories carried lessons. And in this story lies a reminder to carefully handle a potentially deadly, but alluringly beautiful plant; and keep it separate from the food supply. Time passed, food supplies were more readily controlled, and this lesson faded into its story.

The perils of vanity, however, continue to lurk in our midst. The Greek word, *narke* (from the youth's name) is associated with "stupor" (the spell Narcissus felt from his own reflection), and "numbness", a sensation linked to the narcissus plant's narcotic effect. *Narcolepsy* is a condition in which sudden and uncontrolled sleep occurs; a bout of unconsciousness.

Oddly enough, in controlled amounts, the narcissus plant may prove to have a positive effect on health in the modern world. In medical studies, scientists have isolated a toxic substance from the bulb of the narcissus plant which may effect an enzyme believed to be linked to Alzheimer's disease. To remember the stories may be our best medicine of all.

CHAPTER NINE

WONDERING OUTSIDE
THE BOX

Men love to wonder, and that is the seed of science
~ Ralph Waldo Emerson

S cientists contemplate, speculate, ponder and…muse; they too receive inspiration from the Mousai, the Muses of ancient Greece. Scientists form opinions, interpret signs, and establish foundations for theoretical beliefs. Medical science offers a *prognosis*, "a forecasting of the probable course and outcome of a disease, especially of the chances of recovery". Meteorologists *forecast* the weather by analyzing data and determining a likely pattern; and seismologists *predict* earthquakes. Scientists investigate, observe, and test boundaries. They experiment and fail; experiment and find success. They reach logically predictable conclusions, and fortuitously stumble upon astounding discoveries through sheer coincidence and utter dumb luck.

A STORY OF CONTRASTING THEORIES

Science tells a story, and like many stories, it follows a pattern of adaptation. Concepts are modified, abandoned, and replaced with new and improved, more relevant ideals; broadening views and producing other options. Long ago two contrasting theories clashed, and a story with dire consequences unfolded. During the 4th century BCE Greek philosopher Aristotle proclaimed Earth was the center of the universe and all planets, including the sun and moon, revolved around Earth. This he based on several suppositions; one being that Earth must be stationary, for if Earth rotated we would surely fly off its surface into the heavenly ether of space. Aristotle's arguments were quite convincing and his geocentric theory was accepted as most probable.

The idea of a sun-centered universe (the heliocentric model wherein the sun is center and the planets, including Earth, rotate around it) was suggested in the next century by astronomer Aristarchus. His contrarian view did not gather widespread support, and because it did not conform to the current religious teachings Aristarchus's theory was denounced as impiety. Thus Aristotle's geocentric model held its place in history for many more centuries.

Further support for Aristotle's geocentric model came in the 2nd century, when Claudius Ptolemy, the renowned Roman astronomer who compiled *Almagest* (a classical scientific catalog of stars and constellations), supported it. Backed by the powerful Roman Catholic church, acceptance of Ptolemaic theory was solidified. The Church believed Scripture suggested the sun was in constant motion while Earth remained in one place...yet the controversy would not die.

During the Middle Ages, a thousand years after Aristarchus first proposed a heliocentric model, renowned scientists Copernicus, Galileo, and Kepler backed his radical theory of a sun-centered universe. The concept began to take root...and grew in acceptance. New data was uncovered. Previously unknown secrets of the universe were revealed through technological advances. Galileo's 17th century improvements to the newly invented telescope enabled him to view the heavens as never before possible. He concluded that not only were there predictable and cyclical patterns in the sky, but contrary to popular belief, the sun rotated while Earth revolved around the sun...Earth was not the center of the universe after all. Galileo's outspoken support of the controversial heliocentric model, then credited to Copernicus, so offended church leaders he was accused of heresy.

In 1633 a Papal Condemnation against Galileo was issued, stating that: "The proposition that the Sun is the center of the world and does not move from its place is absurd and false philosophically and formally heretical, because it is expressly contrary to Holy Scripture.". The Church's staunch denouncement forced the elderly Galileo to publicly recant his support of the Copernican model; and he was sentenced to spend the remainder of his days imprisoned under house arrest.

It wasn't until the 18th century, with support from the scientific community and endorsement by the Roman Catholic Church, that the heliocentric theory was recognized and commonly accepted. But it took until 1992 (following a papal-requested review of Galileo's 1633 trial) before the Catholic Church issued a formal admission that Galileo's theory had been correct. A 20th century study concluded that, during the time of Galileo's prosecution, theologians misinterpreted the Scriptures which "led them unduly to transpose a question of factual observation into the realm of faith…[and] to a disciplinary measure from which Galileo 'had much to suffer.'".

UNEXPECTED DISCOVERIES

Another longstanding notion—that the world was flat and one could sail off over its edge to meet a horrific end—was also eventually dispelled, in favor of the belief in a round Earth; a global world successfully circumnavigated by members of Magellan's 16th century sailing party. Through perseverance and determination, trial and error, curiosity, and a burning need to know "what makes things tick" humankind continues to discover. An idea or advancement may, at first blush, seem controversial, unusual, or unpopular. When thought fits the design and the solution called forth solves the problem, then its appropriate space in life's puzzle has been found and it is snapped into being.

Great strides have been made while searching for something else, or when attention was focused in another direction. Ideas appear out of the blue, on their own terms and in their own time…or do they? Have they been hovering there all along, merely unnoticed; invisible to our narrow view, waiting until we are ready to openly receive the newly found possibilities? Guided by memories of long ago solutions always arrive right on schedule, when the timing is right to fill yet another marker in the space of humankind's story. We, by our very nature, stand fast and assuredly ask not only "Why?" but "Why not?".

Through perseverance, patience, humility, compassion, and grace some succeed where others fail. Alexander Fleming devoted much of his time in the early 20th century attempting to develop a wonder drug which could combat bacterial disease and infection. But it was not until he noticed a mold growing in a used petri dish contaminated from a previous experiment that he shifted the focus of his research. By further investigating the properties of this "accidental experiment" Fleming isolated a mold which would be used a decade later in the life-saving antibiotic penicillin drug.

Christopher Columbus, 15th century explorer, is credited with discovering America; more by happenstance than by design. Columbus was looking for a trade route to Asia (the Indies). Through miscalculation he believed sailing west and traveling around the world would be a shorter route to Asia than if he followed previously established routes. He sailed west…and the rest is history. Columbus stumbled upon the New World, landing in the Bahamas and Hispaniola. He believed he had reached his charted destination, but discovered instead he had reached the Caribbean islands and mainland South America; not at all what he had been searching for. As luck would have it, discoveries made during excursions under Columbus's command, and voyages by other explorers, generated enough excitement in Europe to fuel a wave of expeditions to the Americas, and opened up a world of possibilities.

Explorers investigate the unknown. They are risk takers and keen observers who recognize that following an obscure lead or inkling could result in the discovery of a valuable scientific advancement. They read between the lines and uncover clues, have faith, and press onward. They are heroes on a quest, determined to succeed.

Scientists too are explorers, delving into the unknown, retracing steps, searching for a better way. The keen eye of science has always observed its natural surroundings. Many stories pay homage to nature's elements, intermingling common objects, and laying out a mind map for those willing (and open) to follow its trail.

ALONG COMES A SPIDER

Spiders are ancient weavers and spinners whose form has changed little through time; some found fossilized in amber dated to an existence millions of years ago. In Greek mythology the mortal woman Arachne ("arachnid") boasted she could weave as skillfully as Athena, goddess of wisdom and war and patroness of craftsmen and weavers. Displeased with such arrogant claims, the goddess Athena warned Arachne there would be consequences for her insolence. Athena challenged Arachne to demonstrate her claim of superior skill in a contest between them. Each woman sat at a loom and masterfully guided a flow of thread to create a wondrous tale woven in tapestry.

Athena recreated the glorious story of her contest against the god Poseidon to win the honor of Athens, her namesake city. But Arachne chose to mock and belittle the gods by weaving scenes of their failings, depicting them as fools. Athena conceded that the quality of Arachne's finished work was flawless, but her blatant disrespect toward the gods would not be tolerated. In anger Athena tore apart Arachne's tapestry and touched the young woman's forehead, instilling in her guilt and shame so powerful that Arachne could not bear the distress of it, and hanged herself. Seeing her dangling by the rope Athena took pity on the young woman and, rather than allow her to perish, turned Arachne into a spider to continue a lifetime of skillfully spinning and weaving her glorious masterpieces in a web of her own silken thread.

Humankind has turned nature's spider web into creations of our own design. Some tribal cultures use readily available spider silk to weave fishing nets and small carrying bags. In 2009 an extraordinary cloth was woven from the silk of golden orb spiders, and put on display at the American Museum of Natural History in New York City. Raw silk spun by the golden orb spider has the natural yellowish color of gold, well suited for this beautifully artistic creation. It took a team of 70 people four years to gather enough spider silk to produce this remarkable fabric.

Web silk is strong and pliable, resilient, waterproof, and adhesive. Its versatility is being studied and tested for feasibility in developing a synthetic silk with properties which emulate spider-produced silk. Practical uses are envisioned for a variety of medical and industrial applications: strong flexible bandages, nerve growth support, protective clothing, durable ropes and netting.

Spider webs and cob webs have been used in folk remedies to aid healing and reduce bleeding on wounds and cuts. Thousands of known spider species produce protein-based silken threads, rich in the blood clotting agent vitamin K. Vitamin K helps strengthen and support capillary walls, and is an ingredient found in modern-day topical creams used to treat "spider veins"—varicose veins—small blood vessels forming a web-like pattern visible through the skin.

SPIDER-MAN, SPIDER-GOAT, AND CHARLOTTE

W hat was once considered impossible now seems within reach; a mythic pattern repeated as ancient stories move from fantastic metaphorical tales to applied cultural truths. In myth, Arachne was completely transformed from human to spider by the goddess Athena. Strange tales are told of characters changing between animal and human forms. Encounters with men turning into werewolves, and vampires turning into bats have long been popular fantasy, but a more recent story weaves its way into our lives as cleverly as Arachne spun her silken thread.

In an early 1960s comic book from the Marvel franchise we were introduced to the world of Peter Parker... Spider-Man. As a teenager Peter was bitten by a radioactive spider and, though he retained human form, he gained super-human abilities; characteristics of an arachnid. Empowered with a spider's proportional strength and agility Peter Parker, as Spider-Man, could cling to surfaces. His web spinning ability was modified from one of a spider's time-consuming, meticulous task which relied on prey to become entangled in his trap, to a skillful ability to quickly cast a web outward and immediately ensnare the bad guy during crime-fighting capers; much to our amusement.

Perhaps mutant human web spinners are best left to the imagination of creative storytellers, but "Spider-Goat" does exist. On the outside this animal looks like any other goat.

Scientists have created an internal mutation by splicing a spider's silk-producing gene into a female goat's DNA. When the female goat gives birth and lactates, silk protein is produced in the milk, solidified by exposure to air, and collected. Scientists envision practical applications for the newly processed silk; with potential use as medical sutures and binding agents, or as ligament replacements.

Years before the comic book character Spider-Man swung onto the scene there was Charlotte, a spider who reversed the role by maintaining her form and displaying humanlike qualities. In 1952, E. B. White's endearing children's book, *Charlotte's Web*, hit the scene. The title character is a clever spider who spun her silk into block letters to form life changing messages: "When the words appeared, everyone said they were a miracle. But nobody pointed out that the web itself is a miracle.".

THE WEB AND THE INTERNET

The book was, of course, referring to the miracle of Charlotte's spider web. But since that time humankind has created its own intricately spun web to carry messages—the World Wide Web—an immense collection of interwoven electronic files and services readily accessed on a daily basis. "The Web" resides on "The Net" or Internet; a worldwide computer network which links smaller networks together to enable an exchange of information. An early platform for the now familiar Internet was developed in the 1960s (well after Charlotte), but it was not until the 1990s that the term "World Wide Web" took hold, spinning its way into our vocabulary and solidifying its place in history as a household mainstay.

Time and again humankind stretches the limits of thinking; reaching beyond established boundaries to create bigger and better, new and improved, unusual and unique discoveries. The World Wide Web—the Internet—continually expands to encompass all we can imagine; offering countless opportunities and endless applications. It is a portal with ready access to volumes of information, the like we have not before seen; timely, magical answers to our quests for new innovations; keys to unlock the mysteries of the universe at our very fingertips.

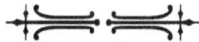

The computer age opened a doorway to an ingenious labyrinth, rivaled only by the intricacies of the mythic one created thousands of years ago by the artisan craftsman, Daedalus. This new labyrinth, traveled with our minds, is as expansive as the scope of our imagination...dare we enter? Like something concocted from the mind of a storyteller... with a mouse to lead the way. A touch of a pad, and our fingertips glide over keys, feeling our way along an imagined hero's clew, navigating through endless passageways, exploring a maze of information: pictures, sounds, words, and symbols.

Yes, we do occasionally encounter the beast within; doing battle, freezing up...crashing. Weary, but not defeated, we reboot, restart, and continue on to face further challenges, exploring more deeply; enriching our lives by devouring those delectable morsels offered in the Web...entangled in its wonder. Tantalizing and innovative applications tempt us as we become caught up in a world so mesmerizing that, if not careful, we might become trapped in the Web while it preys on our insatiable desire for more information.

Intrigued with our newly discovered world we quickly adapt to its culture and learn a new language: website, webinar, webcast, weblog, webmaster. Search engines send out web crawlers (called spiders) to retrieve web pages. In nature, a spider eats not only the prey caught in its web, but devours its own web for nourishment. In turn, the World Wide Web sustains us by spinning a thread of "webfeeds", continually updated, regularly changing bits of information to satisfy the voracious appetite of an online community hungry for knowledge.

COSMIC NET

Long before our Internet evolved, humankind was captivated by the discovery of a heavenly "Net", a clue to what was to come. A quick search on the Internet leads to information about the Southern Hemisphere's constellation Reticulum; commonly referred to as the "Net". It's 17th century discoverer, Isaac Habrecht II, originally named this constellation "Rhombus", presumably because its visible star pattern formed the shape of an equilateral parallelogram. As happens in story adaptation, science blends with and conforms to a broader collective theme.

A century later the French astronomer Nicolas Louis de Lacaille cataloged constellations using naming conventions reflective of the period's cultural focus on industrial, scientific, and artistic instruments. He changed the constellation name "Rhombus" to "Reticle"; a term describing the pattern of focusing crosshairs found inside a telescope eyepiece. (Natural spider silk was the material used to create crosshairs for optical devices—microscopes, telescopes, and gunsights—from the 18th century until the World War II era.)

The name "Reticle" was eventually lengthened to "Reticulum", which described the constellation's inner weblike appearance rather than its outline. In anatomy, reticulum is a network of intercellular fibrous tissue. It is the zoological term used to define the honeycombed cell structure of the second stomach of a ruminant (quadrupeds such as cattle). The slang term "chew the cud" means to think on, or ruminate, which in turn is to ponder or…muse.

Net stretches from sky to everyday life. Mosquito netting keeps out pests, butterfly nets draw in and trap the fluttering beauty, holding it within our sight for a few breathtaking moments longer before it flits away. We literally cast our nets to fish the oceans, and figuratively "cast a wide net" to take in as much information as possible. We network to cultivate contacts, and form a network of computers, radio, and television stations, expanding our communication reach. We value our financial net(worth), and are often quite amused by witnessing the sporting swoosh of…"nothing but net".

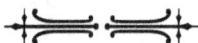

⊢══ ══⊣

Chasing dreams satisfies a fundamental personal need. When there are more no dreams, we cease to exist. And so we sift through endless possibilities to find new stories, breathing them into being through glorious achievement. For dreams to be realized they must be separated from would-be nightmares; a process symbolically reflected through sacred hoops called dreamcatchers. These traditional Native American amulets are woven into a web-like pattern with a center hole, and attached to a frame. Legend tells that good dreams pass through the hole in the center of the web and enter the sleeper's mind while bad dreams get caught within the webbing and disappear with the first rays of the morning light.

THE THEORY OF EVERYTHING

For centuries Native Americans told variations of the legend of Spider Woman, the revered creation goddess who spun the world from her web and chanted and sang all things to life. Did they see, so long ago, what we are now only beginning to learn? Scientists have described the make up of our universe as an immense cosmic spider web, with clusters of galaxies connected by bridge-like filaments and dark matter spun through space. They dream of discovering the "Theory of Everything", a key which unlocks the mystery of how the universe works. Nobel prize winning physicist Albert Einstein spent his later years engrossed in finding a theory which would link gravity and electromagnetism; saying, "I want to know how God created this world. I am not interested in this or that phenomenon, in the spectrum of this or that element. I want to know His thoughts. The rest are details.".

As its name suggests, the Theory of Everything encompasses all forces and all matter. One concept described a cosmic "String Theory" or "Superstring Theory"; postulating that, when broken down, everything in the universe is composed of tiny vibrating strings of energy. Each vibration corresponds to a specific frequency which can be altered; echoes of centuries ago when Pythagoras put forth the theory of the universal monochord and heard the frequencies of the music of the spheres streaming from the heavens.

Modern String Theory (or theories) proposes to explain how the physical universe is held together, and why it works the way it does. The possibilities fascinate not only the scientific community, but open the world's imagination to the wonders found in the "Everywhere".

We are caught up in this universal cosmic web of "God's mind", hungrily, anxiously, and passionately crawling our way through a labyrinth of space and time in search of answers. The myths of Spider Woman, and Athena and Arachne loom before us. We are the weavers of destiny, inheriting their legacy. Will we choose to create a glorious expression of beauty and value, or allow our egos to produce a trivial mockery of fate? All are entrusted to guard the legacy handed down since the beginning of time; adding in unique stitches of our own as embellishment, then passing along this precious heirloom to those yet to come.

As students of life we too muse and wonder outside the box. If science truly is a "systematic knowledge of the physical or material world gained through observation and experimentation", as it is defined, then are we not all scientists, experimenting and observing in this field of everyday life? Can there be any greater expert or authority on the individual self than the one who resides within; the one entrusted with the power to control not only its own physical form, but entrusted to contribute to a harmonious blending with the whole?

Wisdom is gained by observing the results of our participation in life; noting our successes and failures along the way, contributing our findings and conclusions to the greater whole. We make mistakes, errors in judgment, adjust our thinking and actions, and try again; believing a second time or another way may produce a more desirable result. We enjoy great victories (whether contrived, stumbled over, or thrust upon us), and we bask in the glory of our successes. That is the wonder of science.

CHAPTER TEN

Remembering Forward

It's a poor sort of memory that only works backward
~ Lewis Carroll

A sense of knowing that there is more than meets the eye triggers a medley of past ideas and future thoughts meeting in the now; an inherent awareness awakened in some since birth. It is that place tapped into by those extraordinary forward thinkers known as visionaries. They are the ones who walk among us and see endless possibilities. They are the can-doers, why-nots, and what-ifs who, with focused determination, tirelessly and passionately pursue the All.

LEONARDO DA VINCI

Leonardo da Vinci, artist, inventor, scientist; a man whose creations from the 15th and 16th centuries touch our lives today as deeply as if we were present at their unveiling. His priceless artistic masterpieces leave us spell-bound. The captivating eyes and enigmatic smile of the *Mona Lisa* beckon; what mysterious secret does she hide behind her gaze? His *Last Supper*, shrouded in symbolism and intrigue, transforms us from witnessing a sacred event to searching our very souls for signs of deeper meanings; a quiet knowing stirs from within.

Leonardo's rendering of *Vitruvian Man*, an example of the human body's symmetry and proportion (illustrated as one image overlaid upon a second, within a square, within a circle), pays homage to the meticulous work of the first century BCE Roman engineer Marcus Vitruvius Pollio who, through his treatise on architecture, believed structures should follow the form of divinely created proportions embodied in the human physique.

Many of da Vinci's technological inventions were sketched and documented but deemed infeasible to build, and impractical for public use. As unrealized dreams his visions of progress were tucked away; until a time forward when they would be needed, and remembered into being. He envisioned an ornithopter ("bird machine"), a flying machine propelled through the air by the power of human muscle flapping mechanical wings. A lofty idea with serious engineering flaws, perhaps inspired by the ancient story of the clever artisan Daedalus.

Daedalus lost favor with King Minos when he gave Ariadne the secret to maneuver the labyrinth, and Daedalus and his young son Icarus were imprisoned in a high tower. The cunning Daedalus thought to escape through the air and fashioned large wings from the feathers of birds. As the story goes, he strung together feathers and secured them with thread and wax, and curved them like the wings of birds. "… Icarus, my son, I charge you to keep at a moderate height, for if you fly too low the damp will clog your wings, and if too high the heat will melt them.". Alas, we know the fate of the poor Icarus, who recklessly flew too close to the sun. It's heat melted the wax that held together his shapen wings, and down, down he plunged to his death.

This brilliant being—the man da Vinci—expanded his mortal vision to reach a divine level of "all-sight"; gifting humankind with creations from every time. Among his flying machine designs were a glider which floated on the current of the wind, and a helicopter-like machine which resembled a 14th century toy. Such inventions modeled humankind's progressive desire to discover the secret of flight. He crafted weapons of war and destruction: an armored car, giant crossbow, machine for storming walls, submarine, and machine gun.

His more playful creations, a mechanical lion and a robotic knight, have been studied at NASA to aid in the development of robotics used in modern-day space flight. His design for a parachute, based on the workings of a "tent made of linen", was not discovered until well after another had perfected the invention of a parachute. Perhaps da Vinci's earlier idea was floating along the common thread of the collective human unconscious; a design remembered forward, to take its place as a solution when the time for it was right.

THOMAS EDISON

The modern day visionary Thomas Edison ("Wizard of Menlo Park"), is oft quoted as having said: "Genius is one percent inspiration and 99 percent perspiration.". Edison was severely hearing-impaired, had little formal education, yet still held more than a thousand patents in his lifetime; many for improvements to existing concepts. The first patent granted to Edison was for what he called, "a new and useful apparatus named 'Electrographic Vote Recorder and Register'". Edison described it in an 1869 letter to the U.S. Patent Office, saying: "The object of my invention is to produce an apparatus which records and registers in an instant, and with great accuracy, the votes of legislative bodies, thus avoiding loss of valuable time consumed in counting and registering the votes and names, as done in the usual manner...".

Edison's invention worked as described, but his attempts to convince legislators of the immediate value of its practical implementation were unsuccessful. Deemed an invention ahead of its time, legislators did not favor instant vote counting, preferring instead the slow role count vote, during which time filibustering and lobbying for vote changes on issues of interest could be pursued. Edison learned a valuable lesson from his failure to sell the vote recorder, and shifted his focused energy on inventing and developing what he believed to be both innovative and marketable products.

Edison was a man guided by a greater vision. He created functional products useful on a small scale (improvements to the incandescent light bulb) and reached the masses through an entire industry centered around providing affordable electricity; a benefit outlasting generations. In 1882 his commercial power station in lower Manhattan began providing electricity to customers within a square mile radius. Building more and bigger hubs, Edison's contribution soon enabled extended service and greater coverage; touching families, growing businesses, sparking a new modern era. Edison mastered the ability to easily maneuver between present day innovative problem solving and the avant garde world of forward remembering. Like so many others, he transcended the limits of time and tapped into the realm of future possibilities.

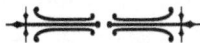

Forward remembering is a gift possessed by the ancients. Inklings of ageless wisdom float in time, waiting for recognition and a call to duty. These precious bits of knowing were woven within fabulous tales to become the myths and legends of the world. Story ("historia") is a recounting of "something". The classical planets, visible with the naked eye, bear the names and exhibit the characteristics carried in tales from long ago.

Many centuries before invention of the telescope enabled humankind to view the physical details of celestial bodies the ancients bestowed upon these planets idiosyncrasies and attributes which carried underlying truths and subconscious traits. Through time these inklings of forward remembering would be validated in discoveries which gave form, substance, and credence to their origin.

SATURN'S MESSAGE

In myth Saturn is the Roman god of agriculture depicted carrying a sickle, who oversees an industry relying heavily on cycles and timing. His namesake planet, observed with the naked eye, appears as a faint orb; the furthest planetary boundary and slowest moving of the classical planets viewable by the ancients. Technology allows us to see rings surrounding this distant orb, a phenomenon Saturn is uniquely associated with...rings which the ancients could not have seen with the naked eye. Saturn's rings were first discovered in the 17th century, after the invention of the telescope.

Galileo turned his eyes to the heavens through the power of a telescopic lens and beheld that which had not before been seen. Although he could not clearly distinguish rings, he saw objects on either side of the planet. Later 17th century astronomers Huygens and Cassini more distinctly observed the identifiable rings and moons of Saturn.

To date, NASA has documented more than 60 confirmed and provisional moons orbiting around their "leader" Saturn. The Roman god Saturn has been compared with the Greek Titan ruler Kronos; some of Saturn's moons are named after Titans, those mythological siblings who ruled before the Olympians.

Ancient astrologer priests associated Saturn (the planet we now know to have an elaborate system of rings), with the process of timing and aging. Here on Earth, nature echoes this lesson. Dendrochronology is the scientific process of dating or aging trees by counting their growth rings. As early as the 4th century BCE, Theophrastus, a student of Aristotle, compiled a detailed botanical account of plants, making note of the annual production of tree rings. A version of his work, *Enquiry into Plants and Minor Works on Odours and Weather Signs*, exists in its 1916 English translation by Sir Arthur Hort.

Nearly 2,000 years after Theophrastus, Leonardo da Vinci noted the correlation between the width of tree rings and climatology (specifically how weather patterns in wet or dry years affected growth). In the early 20th century, Andrew

E. Douglass, known as the "father of dendrochronology", pioneered the study of tree rings as a science and applied its principles to archeology, astronomy, and more.

Forensic aging is another method of counting natural rings; a procedure applied by wildlife biologists on extracted teeth of animals such as: deer, bear, and mountain sheep. Animal teeth produce an annular ring of cementum growth (deposits covering the root of the tooth which can be counted to determine the animal's age); a pattern similar to the annual growth rings formed in the wood of trees. Saturn's association with aging and cycles becomes clearer to us by understanding these natural processes. What did the ancients know...or sense...about that distant planet on the edge of their known universe?

JUPITER'S MESSAGE

Memories, impressions, and thoughts flow forward and back, come into focus and fade away; archived for future use. Patterns repeat as variations on a common theme; unnoticed in the moment yet so easily recognized in hindsight. Attributes of the ancient gods play out in modern times.

Zeus is the Greek god of sky and weather, god of justice, protector of the weak and punisher of wrongdoers. Zeus has been depicted carrying three thunderbolts (forged by Hephaestus and the Cyclopes) which he targeted against humankind's wrongdoings. The first, Zeus cast down as a warning, the second he hurled with dire consequences, and the third strike of his mighty thunderbolt dealt a fatal blow.

Our modern-day justice system has remembered back; tapping into this archetype of Zeus to invoke the "three strikes law", a heavy sentence aimed at repeat offenders. Perhaps the ancients knew humankind would forever yield to the power of Zeus's thunderbolts and etched this eternal warning into their stories.

Zeus, ruler of the Olympian gods, was characterized in story as having sired numerous offspring through his many liaisons with goddesses, nymphs, and mortal women. His Roman counterpart is Jupiter. The planet which bears that name is the largest of the classical planets; named long before any surface details or objects in its surrounding space could be seen. But with the aid of a telescope Jupiter personifies its larger than life mythological namesake.

The planet Jupiter has a powerful magnetic field. A colossal storm known as the Great Red Spot has been observed raging there since the 1800s; an indication of the wrath one might suffer under the swift hand of justice dealt by this king of the gods. More than 60 moons have been discovered orbiting around "father" Jupiter, within a radiation belt of the planet's magnetic field called the Jovian magnetosphere; stretching outward as far as Saturn's orbit. A vast kingdom to rule.

Jove is an early name for the Roman god Jupiter; a nod to his patronage over good fortune. Jovial was a word used to describe this god's influence; those born under his sign were said to be blessed with a merry disposition. A more modern, but somewhat dated exclamation of surprise and emphasis is familiar to many in the expression: "By Jove!"—calling forth the mighty power of Jupiter.

THE OBJECT FORMERLY KNOWN AS PLANET

Our memories drift through the ages recalling impressions of times before and times to come; remembering into being that which is needed in the now, allowing what has served its purpose to fade into the background. Such seems to be the fate of the "planet" Pluto. The 1930 discovery of this outer planet by Clyde Tombaugh of the Lowell Observatory prompted Venetia Burney (a young English schoolgirl with an interest in mythology and knowledge of the solar system) to suggest naming it "Pluto". Some have speculated the planet received its name from the Disney cartoon pup, but that story has been refuted, noting the cartoon character Pluto (previously called Rover) began using this name in 1931—the year after the planet bore that name.

In mythology, the Roman god Pluto was "King of Earthly Riches" who held patronage over wealth. Rich mineral deposits are found beneath the surface of the earth—including those trace amounts of his namesake radioactive element—plutonium. Plutonium was synthesized for military and commercial use in the decade after the planet Pluto's discovery. Harnessing atomic power was a focus of the Manhattan Project during the World War II era. Atomic weaponry gave humankind the power of the gods...and with it the potential to wield destruction and annihilation that rivaled the great battles etched in mythic stories. Pluto's Greek counterpart is Hades, familiar to us as the much feared god who ruled the Underworld—land of the dead. Pluto and Hades are two gods with patronage befitting the power behind the deadly weapons unleashed by humankind's discovery of plutonium.

In astrology, Pluto's influence represents an intense "beneath the surface" transformation. It is the metamorphosis of the caterpillar dissolving into becoming the beautiful butterfly. It is the symbol of the mythical phoenix bird; at the end of its life it burst into flame to be reborn from the ashes of its own funeral pyre. Pluto is an outer planet, unseen by the ancients...but perhaps its powerful energy was felt through the unconscious thread of the Universe. It was discovered and named in a modern decade of deep transformation; an explosive time when experimentation with atomic energy and nuclear fission was underway.

Pluto was classified as a planet, but its status as such became a subject of debate during the decades when the world struggled to reduce its fear-based dependence on nuclear weapons. In 2006 Pluto's status was officially transformed through demotion, and reclassification as "dwarf planet" or "asteroid"; a move which coincided with our time of nuclear disarmament. Plutonium's use was powerful, explosive, and deadly. As the world reacted to its lethal elemental characteristics by downplaying its role, the status of its namesake planet also changed.

Humankind's focus was transformed by the realization that harnessing the power of Pluto produced the potential for global extinction. A planet remembered into view in 1930; called forth to act in a time of deep worldly transformation, then set aside in 2006 to serve a lesser role, perhaps sensing that elevating Pluto to a godly status was a price too high to pay. Did we remember forward in time to save ourselves from annihilation?

One of the world's wealthiest men, Sir Richard Branson, offered his own humorous take on Pluto's demotion. Coinciding with April Fools' Day 2011 a press release was sent out as notification that he had purchased Pluto with the intent to have it reinstated as a planet. This he would accomplish by commissioning the build of an innovative rocket to collect space debris and add it to Pluto's bulk, giving the planet the required mass to be reclassified as a planet by scientific community standards. From Pluto comes the word "plutocracy"…meaning "the rule or power of wealth or of the wealthy". How cleverly appropriate for one of the world's wealthiest men (a plutocrat), to lend his hand to a namesake prank of this magnitude. Bravo, Sir Richard!

THE WORLD OF SCIENCE FICTION

The world of science fiction is rife with visions of forward remembering. The 19th century creative mind of Jules Verne introduced us to the futuristic undersea vessel "Nautilus"; a submarine equipped with luxurious amenities. It was exquisitely bedecked with features which rival anything found on today's finest cruise ships or extravagantly furnished yachts. Verne described the vessel in elaborate detail: a library with wooden bookcases inlaid with fine metalwork, volumes of works in various languages representing the finest achievements in history, literature, and science; a museum of treasured art, paintings by the Old Masters Raphael, da Vinci, and Rubens; and a fully functioning kitchen complete with a "distilling apparatus" to purify drinking water.

Powered by electricity and capable of underwater travel at 50 mph, this literary submarine was painstakingly built in glorious detail, not in a shipyard but in the ingenious workshop of Jules Verne's mind. In Verne's real life world electricity was only beginning to display the scope of its possible uses. It would be another 25 years after publication of

Verne's book, *20,000 Leagues Under the Sea*, before inventors John P. Holland and Simon Lake separately developed submarines which used electric motors for underwater travel and powering torpedoes. Verne's visionary sense of technical science allowed him to springboard into a world far beyond mundane capabilities. His ideas opened a doorway to a future of endless possibilities which manifested in the realm of the practical and took their place among the lives of generations to come.

Another literary luminary, H.G. Wells, commented on the comparison of his own stories with those of earlier works by Jules Verne, saying: "His [Verne] work dealt almost always with actual possibilities of invention and discovery, and he made some remarkable forecasts...but these stories of mine...do not pretend to deal with possible things; they are exercises of the imagination in a quite different field.".

In Wells's *The Time Machine*, the title vehicle was crafted to resemble a rather simplistic chair-like apparatus; he called it a saddle. Wells chose to have us "saddle up" to experience a wondrous adventure alongside the main character, who literally travels by the seat of his pants into the unknown. Many of the characters in this story are "named" by occupation or description: Time Traveller, Psychologist, Provincial Mayor, Editor, Medical Man, Silent Man, and Very Young Man (who said about time travel: "One might get one's Greek from the very lips of Homer and Plato.").

Wells, rather than delve into the workings of some elaborate chamber or concoct a potion to be swallowed, carried us through time on a simple open framework; as if to have us experience (or re-experience) the childlike wonder and thrill of gliding downhill to victory in a home-built soap box derby car. Decades spent exploring the discoveries laid out by Jules Verne and H.G. Wells readied our minds for the incredibly ingenious imagination of Gene Roddenberry and his *Star Trek* creations. His avant garde television series hit the airwaves in 1966, three years before the first man walked on the moon.

Political and social messages aside, *Star Trek* fascinated us with its multitude of futuristic technological gadgets. We watched as the *Star Trek* crew flipped open their communicators (similar in appearance to what would later become an early cell phone design), and Lieutenant Uhura received messages through an earpiece device with an uncanny resemblance to what is a modern-day hands-free headset. The *Star Trek* phaser weapon set on "stun" incapacitates its target like the modern day trademark Taser device used by law enforcement. The duty roster presented to Captain Kirk looks much like our computer tablet pad devices; and those convenient touch-free self-opening sliding doors on the Enterprise ship are now an expectation in modern commercial buildings (sans the cool sound effect).

New episodes of the original *Star Trek* ended 3 years after its debut, but the show had clearly left a deep and lasting impression…enough to carry the original episodes onward into the world of syndication. *Star Trek* developed a cult-like following of devoted fans and played to audiences for years to come, then generated spin off series: *New Generation, Deep Space Nine, Voyager, Enterprise*; even an animated series and several box office movies, all showcasing increasingly fantastic innovations.

Masterful writing and artistic storytelling make imaginative thoughts and fantastic descriptions seem plausible. A visionary senses the presence of an energy lurking in the shadows, transcends time and space, and draws it in to be expressed in some new form. These seers instill in us a desire to believe, create, and dream. Forward remembering triggers a deeper yearning to tap into the knowledge of every time; a fervor with such creative force that we are catapulted through the ages, moving ahead twofold for every look back.

CHAPTER ELEVEN

ALCHEMISTS OF STORY

A man who tells secrets or stories
must think of who is hearing or reading,
for a story has as many versions as it has readers
~ John Steinbeck

Gifted storytellers possess the power to concoct a spell-binding tale; to weave a web of thoughtful contemplation over all who have the courage to listen. The right mix of words sprinkled with a dash of mischief whets the appetite; the tantalizing morsels are digested, and our craving grows. The hunger lingers until that empty space within is satisfied by indulging in another taste of the nourishing vitality cast forth by these skillful wizards. The storyteller obliges by apportioning a measured dose…not too little…not too much… just right.

Storytellers nurture their age old craft; always with a watchful eye in search of the identifiable glow of another teller. And only then do they whisper their secrets on the wind, where they travel to rest in the sacred care of the next teller, until such time as they are passed along to the next. It is the destiny of each storyteller to preserve and polish these precious tales.

Wrapping ideas in well crafted metaphor immortalizes them. The fundamental message thrives and gains character from life's experiences, yet always bears a glimmer of its original form. Ideas live and grow, transformed by current influence; a vague recognition, an inkling from another time remains. The world of metaphor is a universally understood language, a celebrated litany of pure thought, appreciated by those who grasp its subtle meaning.

THE STORY OF PERCEPTION

Our personal stories reflect out into the world. Life becomes a series of collective perceptions, strung together by descriptive language and a flurry of imaginative action; revised, adapted, improvised, and tweaked as the day goes on. Social change spreads and words take on new meanings to match the underlying shift. "Cool" was once a measure of temperature or mood, but in the latter decades of the 20th century it became a state of being. This one simple word "cool" possessed the power to determine one's status; swaying opinions and controlling destinies. It was a powerful accolade, a label affirming one's acceptance into a revered circle; giving one recognition merely by association with its new meaning.

If imagination were an artist's canvas it would hold an endless palette of colorful expression. Each flash of remembering would be transformed into an energized brushstroke—softly flowing or sharply harsh and dramatically poignant—all taking shape in worldly form. Innovative works of breathtaking art, a musical interlude, a captivating story, a towering structure; each creation unfolds from rearranged thoughts of other times layered in the Now.

We, the soulful artists, are fast at work, consumed with adding to, erasing and modifying these visions as if some invisible hand guides every stroke…the next more brilliant than the last. Our world is an endless canvas of creativity, growth, awareness, and remembering. Tapping into the knowledge of the ages opens the source of that which has existed throughout eternity, waiting to be once again breathed into being.

THE SAME OLD STORY

We've grown accustomed to hearing the same old story in new and exciting ways; through parallel plots and fresh scenes advanced by the movie and entertainment industry. Remakes and adaptations of tales from long ago and far away have been pivotal in funneling age old lessons. Our everyday lives collide with story; tales torn from the pages of yesteryear and tomorrow. We need only use our imagination to appreciate them.

George Lucas, an ingenious filmmaker, drew inspiration from the works of mythologist and scholar Joseph Campbell, who spoke of the hero's journey as a "call to adventure" fraught with challenges, heartache, divine meetings, and glorious accomplishment; life's sacred initiation and rite of passage. The depth of Lucas's characters and his intricately woven storylines masterfully bring to life reminiscences of heroes and great battles found in familiar tales. The *Indiana Jones* adventures and the *Star Wars* saga transport us into magically unfolding realms of heroes and villains—good versus evil; from noble quests and reluctant undertakings, through dangers and into wondrous worlds of new, yet somehow familiar, scenarios.

Characters in *The Matrix* movies have names torn from Greek and Roman myth: Morpheus, Oracle, and Neo. In stories of old, Morpheus was a god of dreams who created visions in the mind, and in the movie Morpheus introduced Neo to a vision of an alternate reality. In ancient Greece, prophecies were handed down at the site of the Oracle (as in the Oracle at Delphi). *The Matrix* movie cast a character named Oracle...she who was sought out to provide insight. Neo (from the Greek word for "new") is used in modern language as a prefix meaning "revival" or "relating to", as in "neoclassic" or "neophyte". Neo, *The Matrix* character, is recruited as the newest team member, the unaware novice who is told to "wake up and follow the white rabbit" (a nod to the Lewis Carroll world of Alice and her many adventures in Wonderland).

The comedy *Bill and Ted's Excellent Adventure* takes us on a wild ride through history alongside two high school goof-offs. Crammed together inside a telephone booth the characters travel through the "circuits of time"; humankind's universal thread. An encounter with Socrates in ancient Greece, a clash with Napoleon in 1805 Austria, an alliance with Billy the Kid in the American Old West, a bizarre face to face with themselves; a brief trip to Future and return to Now all traveled via a dial of the telephone.

In the first installment of the *Back to the Future* trilogy, Marty McFly crossed time riding in a modified DeLorean automobile powered by the chemical element plutonium. When the DeLorean's land speed reached 88 mph the ve-hicle propelled into hyperdrive, transporting itself and its oc-cupants into another time period. Was the number 88 merely a coincidence, or based in mythology?

The planet Mercury completes its orbit around the sun in 88 days. The DeLorean was the color of mercury. The Roman god Mercury (Greek Hermes) oversees travelers and communication. In myth, Hermes frequently crossed among worlds, from his home on Olympus into the Underworld and throughout the earthly world of humankind.

In the movie we are shown that tampering with events in time, however well-intended, sent forth ripples which delivered shockwaves with serious consequences to other times. A lesson in the value of innovation and adaptation arose when a tried and true key element of past success was unavailable. Marty got stuck in the year 1955…lacking enough plutonium to propel the DeLorean into its hyperdrive return trip… big problem! The seemingly impossible is accomplished when Marty cleverly maneuvered his vehicle into the energy path of a conveniently well-placed movie lightning strike. (Was that Zeus helping out?)

Life is a series of intermittent adaptations. We learn that, although circumstances may look the same on the surface, applying previously successful solutions may not always produce the desired result. Each situation is unique, none a precise replica of the past. History has proven its worth as a valuable guide, but Now requires focus and its own distinctive twist on the theme; the solution to "everything" is found "everywhere". Perspective changes in the blink of an eye. Shades of familiar characters from story step into roles seen throughout our daily routine, adapting from one scenario to the next.

TAKE ME OUT TO THE BALLGAME

We are fans; fanatics in awe of heroes. Many of us enjoy the game of baseball—America's favorite pastime—but have you experienced a game set amidst a backdrop of the ancient Roman Colosseum? Story layered over time unfolds a new version…teaming the likes of Theseus, the Minotaur, and Zeus; with appearances by an array of characters from tales of long ago and far away. "Take me out to the ballgame!" is the magical phrase which transports us to this field of dreams; devoted fans flocking to a stadium, hoping for a personal encounter with a modern-day hero. We pay homage to these divine idols, buying our way into their presence with a ticket that gives its bearer the privilege of a seat among thousands of spectators in the makeshift Colosseum.

We make an offering to Mnemosyne, goddess of memory and remembrance, before taking our assigned seat; acquiring memorabilia—souvenirs through which this moment in time will be etched in our mind. We ask for divine intervention, praying that we will be one of the "chosen", favored by the gods on this special day. If so, they will send a stray baseball our way; a very special treasure hit off the club of a hero. "What are the odds?", we wonder as we check the distance from our seat to the playing field. We smile and surmise that the cost of the ticket was well worth it; from our viewpoint we are sure to gain an advantage.

The labyrinth of the infield stretches before us; we take a moment to survey its path, unlike poor Theseus who entered into the Minotaur's lair under quite different circumstances. Flanked by foul line markings the hero's journey is clearly defined, a single perilous route leads round a diamond, and onward to home; victory for those who successfully complete this quest. Caught up in the reverie we give thanks to the Muses, those daughters of Mnemosyne who most assuredly inspired this glorious spectacle of amusement we are about to witness. Anticipating the beginning of the action we settle in with our ballpark snacks, imagining the presence of those ancient gods who supped on nectar and ambrosia while they watched the spectacle of humankind's challenges played out in life's arena. Our thoughtful contemplation is broken as the home team charges onto the field to defend its territory.

With the thundering voice of Zeus the umpire commands, "PLAY BALL!"; all eyes turn as the battle begins. The Minotaur, garbed in pitcher's uniform, looms menacingly on the mound…centered within the labyrinth of the infield. Prepared for battle the opposing team sends its lead-off hitter into the batter's box. We size him up and down, trying to determine whether he is the hero Theseus, or merely one of the many victims chosen by lot to be served up at home plate as a sacrificial feast for the Minotaur. Anxiously we await his fate as he makes his stand, proudly and defiantly displaying his weapon of choice—a wooden bat. If he is aligned with the gods his weapon will be strong and true; perhaps forged with the skill of Hephaestus.

Movement within the labyrinth draws the crowd's attention back to the Minotaur. Like a bull pounds its hoof before a charge the pitcher digs his foot into the dirt on the mound; feasting his eyes on his mark at the plate. The windup…the pitch. With fixated stare the batter zeroes in on the fast-approaching orb, and times the swing of his club to send the baseball crashing into the sky. Spectators and players alike hold their breath; all eyes follow its path to see whether or not it will run afoul of the designated boundaries. The signal is given for foul ball, a sigh of relief from some, as the players resume their positions.

The dance between the Minotaur and the hero repeats again and again until "fair ball" is determined. This time the gasps from the crowd alert us that the baseball has traveled into an abyss of open ground, landing far beyond the Minotaur's reach. The batter charges forth to run the course of the labyrinth. He follows the hero's clew etched into the field; a pathway worn from the pounding feet of so many heroes who have gone before. Blessed with fleet of foot, he safely reaches first base…a small oasis bringing temporary respite from the angry beast. Too dangerous to continue further, he catches his breath and contemplates his next move.

Another enters the batter's box. The Minotaur pays him little attention, still fixated on the runner at first base. The hero on first taunts the Minotaur, stepping away from the safety of the bag. As he prepares to steal forward to second we wonder if he will survive the Minotaur's relentless attack. Are we witnessing hero or victim? The runner edges toward second, pauses, and quickly retreats, diving toward the safety of first base as he meets the threatening stare from the Minotaur.

Attention returns to the batter at the plate. The Minotaur's next pitch misses its mark and rolls too far away...our hero on first easily steals second! From his new vantage point our hero bides his time and plots his next move. His prayers are answered when the batter at the plate delivers a sacrifice fly. The gods must be smiling down on him. No time to lose. He seizes the opportunity and rounds third base with no thought of stopping; narrowly escaping the wrath of the Minotaur as he slides across home plate, just ahead of the throw...safe!

Amid the cheers of the crowd this smiling hero collects his boon...high-fives from teammates and a precious run scored for the team. The battle-worn pitcher hangs his head and glances over at his bullpen to see the looming figures of caged relief pitchers; two fresh beasts in warm up action, ready to charge in at the king's command. One hero has already outwitted the Minotaur, yet this beast lives on... next batter up, hero or victim...another's journey into the labyrinth begins.

The Minotaur winds up, takes deadly aim and unleashes his fury at his new mark. The batter stands frozen and stares as, swoosh…just off the corner of the plate; too close to call, no swing. The batter glances at the home plate umpire; a theatrical motion of the arm accompanied by the execution of his call…as if mighty Zeus, god of justice himself has cast down the first thunderbolt…STRIKE ONE! The batter regains his composure and prepares for the next attack. A perfect throw, a strong swing…but too late; the ball carries past the batter. He hears the deadening thud as it pounds into the glove of the catcher. Thundering down comes the arm of Zeus…STRIKE TWO! The dazed batter stands once more to face the wrath of the pitcher and wonders, "Who is this beast of a man on the mound?".

The Minotaur is refreshed knowing that the batter is wounded by two strikes. But wounded prey is dangerous, and the focused pitcher readies to finish him off…with a curve ball. He grips the ball and runs his fingers over its familiar cowhide cover, feeling the 88 inches of hand-stitched red thread encircling the baseball; binding it together. Could this thread be a remnant of the hero's clew laid down in myth by Theseus? Is this the key to victory? Or does it herald the arrival of yet another god?

Eighty-eight inches of thread…88 days for the planet Mercury to orbit the sun. Roman Mercury is the Greek Hermes; the shapeshifter. Perhaps that scoundrel has entered the game to trick us! Bemused, we wonder…"Is the pitcher the Minotaur…or is HE the true Hero?". We look to Zeus for answers. As in the dilemma of Apollo's stolen cattle surely he, with his gift of prophecy, can sort this out. Our mind wanders back over the previous plays in search of a clue.

We smile as we remember the lines from an old Abbott and Costello comedy routine: "Who's on first…What's on second…I Don't Know's on third…The pitcher's name? Tomorrow.". Ah yes, Hermes is the trickster god; and with this thought we turn our attention back to the game just in time to see Zeus cast down his final fatal thunderbolt… "STRIKE THREE!"…the signal for the defeated batter to leave the field of play, a victim of the Minotaur. As for identifying the hero in this tale…now that is a matter of perspective; it all depends on which team you are rooting for. In baseball, as in life, one person's hero is another's beast.

THE PHILOSOPHER'S STONE

Ancient alchemists were obsessed with discovering the secret formula which held the power to change lead into gold. They yearned to uncover eternal youth and capture immortality. So focused on tangible earthly elements were they that they overlooked the key to unlocking the mystery of the ages. It was there beside them all along…as it has been since the beginning of time. Story is the true philosopher's stone. It is the magical elixir that keeps us young at heart, and is more precious than gold or silver. Story is timeless… and ageless. Story has always been…and will always be. We are the modern-day alchemists; storytellers entrusted with this eternal sacred gift.

Passed down from generation to generation, crossing cultures, myths and stories—old and new—live on through those of us who honor their presence. With every breath we are reintroduced to an old friend whose theme plays out in new scripts to deliver a timeless message, and re-awaken a world to endless possibilities with a renewed sense of fascination. The story you remember into being, the one breathed into life, has the power to change the universe. Be mindful what you reach for inside your bag of tricks, for gathering the precise ingredients to conjure a nourishing selection of endlessly creative tales—a cure for what ails us—is a delicate formula. Through stories we find our sense of purpose; they are the mythic patterns that shape our lives.

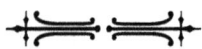

BIBLIOGRAPHY

Aristotle. *Poetics*. Translated by S. H. Butcher.
Project Gutenberg Ebook #1974. Released, 2008.

Baum, L. Frank. *The Wonderful Wizard of Oz*.
Project Gutenberg Ebook #55. Released, 2008.

Browning, Elizabeth Barrett. *Sonnets From the Portuguese*.
Project Gutenberg Ebook #2002. Released, 2002.

Bulfinch, Thomas. *Bulfinch's Mythology*. Introduction and
Notes by Charles Martin. New York: Barnes & Noble
Classics, 2006.

Campbell, Joseph. *The Hero With a Thousand Faces*.
Novato, CA: New World Library, 2008.

Campbell, Joseph. *The Power of Myth*. With Bill Moyers.
New York: Doubleday, 1988.

Carroll, Lewis. *Alice's Adventures in Wonderland*. Project
Gutenberg Ebook #11. Released, 2008. Updated, 2011.

Cotterell, Arthur & Storm, Rachel. *The Illustrated Encyclopedia of World Mythology.* New York: Metro Books, 2010.

Grimm, Jacob & Wilhelm. *Household Tales.* Translated by Margaret Hunt. Project Gutenberg Ebook #5314. Released, 2004. Updated, 2006.

Heifetz, Milton D. and Tirion, Wil. *A Walk Through the Heavens.* New York: Cambridge University Press; 2004.

Homer and Hesiod. *Hesiod, The Homeric Hymns, and Homerica.* Edited by Hugh G. Evelyn-White. Project Gutenberg Ebook #348. Released, 2008.

Lang, Andrew, ed. *The Red Fairy Book.* Project Gutenberg Ebook #540. Released, 2009.

Ovid. *The Metamorphoses of Publius Ovidius Naso in English blank verse Vols. I&II.* Translated by J. J. Howard. Project Gutenberg Ebook #28621. Released, 2009.

Plato. *The Republic.* Translated by Benjamin Jowett. Project Gutenberg Ebook #1497. Released, 2008.

Pollio, Marcus Vitruvius. *The Ten Books on Architecture.* Translated by Morris Hicky Morgan. New York: Elibron Classics unabridged facsimile of the edition published in 1914 by Harvard University Press, Cambridge, 2004.

Raff, Jeffrey. *Jung and the Alchemical Imagination.* Lake Worth, FL: Nicolas-Hayes, 2000.

Sabin, Frances E. *Classical Myths That Live Today.*
New York: Silver Burdett Company, 1940.

Smith, William, ed. *Dictionary of Greek and Roman Antiquities.* Oxford: C.C. Little and J. Brown, 1853.
Digitized by Google, 2007.

Verne, Jules. *Twenty Thousand Leagues Under the Sea.*
Introduction and Notes by Victoria Blake. New York:
Barnes & Noble Classics, 2005.

Virgil. *Aeneid.* Project Gutenberg Ebook #228.
Released, 2008.

Wells, H.G. *The Time Machine and the Invisible Man.*
Introduction and Notes by Alfred Mac Adam. New York:
Barnes & Noble Classics, 2008.

White, E.B. *Charlotte's Web.* New York:
Harper Collins, 2004.

Wilkinson, Philip & Philip, Neil. *Visual Reference Guides: Mythology.* New York: Metro Books, 2010.

Wright, Craig. *The Maze and the Warrior.* Cambridge:
Harvard University Press, 2001.

www.ingramcontent.com/pod-product-compliance
Lightning Source LLC
Chambersburg PA
CBHW022106280326
41933CB00007B/275